Adventures of a Cheap Antiquer

by Arline Beitler

AVON
PUBLISHERS OF BARD, CAMELOT AND DISCUS BOOKS

ADVENTURES OF A CHEAP ANTIQUER is an original publication of Avon Books. This work has never before appeared in book form.

AVON BOOKS
A division of
The Hearst Corporation
959 Eighth Avenue
New York, New York 10019

Copyright © 1979 by Arline Beitler
Published by arrangement with the author.
Library of Congress Catalog Card Number: 78-64739
ISBN: 0-380-42804-0

All rights reserved, which includes the right to reproduce this book or portions thereof in any form whatsoever. For information address Carole Abel, Literary Agent
160 West 87th Street
New York, New York 10024

First Avon Printing, March, 1979

AVON TRADEMARK REG. U.S. PAT. OFF. AND IN OTHER COUNTRIES, MARCA REGISTRADA, HECHO EN U.S.A.

Printed in the U.S.A.

The Tell-Tale Signs of Antique Fever:

Your heart beats faster at the sight of cut glass, ornate picture frames, primitive sculpture and enamel vases.

Your palms sweat at the thought of oriental figurines, antique jewelry, bone china and brass fixtures.

You find yourself disgusted with mass produced, poor quality workmanship.

The Antiques Bug Needn't Send You to the Poorhouse.

You can uncover beautiful finds if you know where to look at rummage sales, bazaars, garage sales, Swap and Shops, thrift shops and flea markets.

You can outwit possessive antique dealers and quick thinking auctioneers.

Your petty cash budget can buy you valuable antiques.

When Arline Beitler moved from a cramped three room apartment to a spacious English Tudor house, the challenge of filling the emptiness on a limited budget led her to unexpected encounters with second-hand elegance in neighbor's backyards and farmers' markets, all for prices ranging from 25¢ to $50.00. Hunting for the best buys is fun—and profitable.

Learn How to Budget for, Bargain for, Buy and Sell Antiques, <u>Cheaply!</u>

For my family, Stan, Steve and Norma

Contents

1. How I Fell into the Antiques Trap — 9
2. Where to Buy — 17
3. How to Budget — 29
4. Antiques Shops — 39
5. Garage Sales — 53
6. Just Plain Folks — 69
7. Auctions — 79
8. Flea Markets — 89
9. Bazaars — 97
10. Rummage Sales — 105
11. Thrift Shops — 117
12. Raiding the Rubbish — 127
13. Fairs, Farmers' Markets (and Coney Island) — 135
14. Collectors' Clubs — 143
15. Swap and Shop — 151
16. Antiques Shows — 163
17. Museums — 171
18. Selling Your Antiques — 177
19. Potpourri — 185

1
How I Fell into the Antiques Trap

About a dozen years ago I moved from a medium-sized three-room city apartment to a moderate-priced English Tudor house in the suburbs, the kind of place that was built when people could still afford large families. There were eight tremendous rooms and a spacious wood-paneled basement. Even the upstairs bathroom was banquet-sized. I especially loved the ten-foot-high sunken living room with Tudor beamed ceilings, a brick fireplace, stucco walls, and one giant, partially stained-glass window. I decided I would furnish it like Henry VIII's throne room!

While the euphoria of possession was at its height, I was ambitious to fill my beautiful new home with the best furniture money could buy. All that was missing was the money. My husband and I had ordered rugs and a couch, only to find that the payments would eat up the rest of our youth.

It took a few weeks of adjustment to the neighborhood, the neighbors, and the neighbors' houses for me to realize that I was surrounded by a wide range of partially empty homes and that being poor assured me of instant friendship with my neighbors. I was welcomed like a long-lost sister by all the young matrons who tramped through my barren rooms.

However, knowing I wasn't alone didn't fully ease the emptiness around me. The house was beginning to feel like a great yawning mouth. I had to feed it something; not any old thing, either—it was a special house with special appetites. What could I do?

Fortunately, I'm sociable and I keep my eyes open. I was invited from house to house for coffee and cake, and I got a rundown on what other people were doing to beat the money rap. I soon observed that a few homes looked fuller and more dazzling than the rest. They contained high-quality furniture interspersed with expensive-looking antiques.

I didn't know anyone well enough to ask, "What did you really pay for that expensive-looking table?" or "Who gave you those valuable antique cabinets?" or "How did you manage the chandelier on your husband's salary?"

Two of the women in my neighborhood seemed to be the trend setters. Here are some of the lovely things they had: carved, reupholstered Victorian couches; golden oak turn-of-the-century pieces ranging from bookcase-desks to pedestals to china closets; quaint Singer sewing machine cabinets that doubled as furniture; a Victorian organ; and an elaborate brass bed. In addition, there were accent pieces that ran the gamut from pressed glass to oak medicine cabinets to china-headed dolls.

My curiosity was overwhelming. How had they done all this on a standard middle-class salary? I wasn't a collector then, but I did recognize fine antiques. How had these average housewives acquired such outstanding furnishings without going to debtors' prison?

I learned the answer traumatically one rainy morning while I was vainly trying to amuse my then four-year-old daughter, Norma. The phone call pealed through my shattered nerves like a deliverance from heaven.

"Come over for coffee and see my basement; we just

finished the paneling." It was Janet, one of my trend setters. I never refused a summons from her.

"I have to bring Norma; is that all right?" I held my breath.

"Sure. She can play in Jody's room. Jody's at school."

The absent Jody had a room as delightful as the rest of this marvelously furnished house. Norma was thrilled to play there as Janet and I went to inspect the basement.

The new panels were a warm-toned golden oak type of wood grain. They lit up the subterranean room. There were also two marvelous brass and carnival glass fixtures suspended from the ceiling. But the most magic light of all came from floor and table lamps of brass, bamboo, and wrought iron, with little touches of crystal, leaded inserts of stained glass, beading, frail old silken shades, and so on, each dating from the early age of electricity.

Janet had superbly blended rattan and other casual furniture throughout the room, all of it built at a time when durability and comfort were a way of life.

"I can't believe it's a basement! It's like the royal suite at the Waldorf!" My voice sounded shrill, distant, and full of envy.

Janet laughed modestly to cover a spreading glow of pride. I had picked up an iridescent ashtray and was nervously stroking its cool slippery surface, trying to muster the nerve to ask her if I too could do this on my limited budget (thereby opening the possibility of financial revelations she might be reluctant to make), when a splintering crash echoed above our heads.

I almost dropped the ashtray. Something had happened to Norma. Worse yet, Norma had done something to the house.

We raced upstairs to find the apple of my eye in the living room, standing erect (not horizontal) without any visible bumps, bruises, or bleeding. Directly below her were the shattered pieces of a glass (crystal?!)

something-or-other. Norma seemed traumatized. Her eyes, which seemed the only living part of her, reflected her anxieties about the punishment to come.

"Oh, look at the poor thing." Without a thought for the breakage, Janet scooped up my darling and smothered her with kisses.

"But your—what is it?—"

"Candy dish—don't worry—"

"It looks like cut glass—an antique!—oh!! . . ." I saw dollars floating away from me into space. I saw my family's reputation shattered and lying on the floor ("Don't invite the Beitlers, their kids are housewreckers."). The only thing that could save me was an instant heart attack.

"In the first place, it's not cut glass; it's pressed, which is less expensive. And I didn't get it at an antiques shop; I got it at a thrift shop years ago for fifty cents."

I wouldn't believe her. "Nonsense!"

Janet answered my protests with, "I'll show you the difference between cut and pressed glass." And she took me on a Cook's tour of glass throughout her home. I saw cut, pressed, pattern, Depression, art, carnival, hand-blown, mold-blown, etched, and other types of old glass. And the prices she quoted! (without my asking): a dollar at the Salvation Army, a quarter at a house sale, fifty cents at a church sale; she even had five-cent and ten-cent items, with almost nothing that had cost above five dollars except furniture and a few good-quality antiques. She had bought most of her things about three to five years earlier, when prices had been exceptionally low.

"But you can still find bargains," Janet insisted. Without hesitation, she let me in on all her secrets. Most of her furniture had come from the Salvation Army, and had been incredibly cheap, although a few pieces had been bought through other outlets. The prices ranged anywhere from five dollars to fifty, with most under twenty-five, including antiques. I smiled inside as I listened to the pride in her voice. Here she was, so pleased with her merchandising skills, and there I'd been, afraid to ask anything as personal as, "What did you pay for it?"

That was twelve years ago, and prices have since skyrocketed. But there are still options available to you through the various sales, shops, and open markets throughout the country. I'll talk about them in later chapters.

I soon began to visit the Salvation Army stores, and this was where my obsession with antiques started. By the time I realized I didn't have enough money to be a collector, I was already hooked. I had begun to feel inexplicable pangs of yearning for strange old pieces that were often cracked, chipped, tarnished, rickety, and rotten, and which I had begun to adore with the same unreasonable passion which Shakespeare's Titania had lavished on donkey-headed Bottom.

Then someone tipped me off to the classified section of our local newspapers, and the garage sale. New doors were opening. I was learning to pay less and buy more. The obsession grew. My living patterns changed: more of my time was spent on antiques, and less on my family. I ran from one musty hyperallergenic antique shop to another. I passed in and out of garage sales, house sales, estate sales, and rummage sales. I spent too many hours at noisy, smoky auctions. I began to not notice the smell of dried human sweat that's characteristic of thrift shops.

I metamorphosed from a needy suburban housewife to a greedy, grasping, and perennially money-conscious collector. In addition to the cash I didn't really have for antiques, I spent $59.80 a year on the local newspapers so that I could slobber over the "Merchandise for Sale" section of the classified ads. Obviously I needed money.

Where did I get it? My secret source has been my household and sundries budget. I've managed to save money out of the same amount that was never enough for me before. I've resisted the little expensive indulgences, like eating lunch out and buying clothes, that I used to think I needed. You can do it too. Further on I'll discuss it in detail.

Love of antiques must be the overall motivation. I'll tell you how to buy them the way dealers do. You can utilize many, if not all, of their sources. I'll tell you where to shop and how to bargain, word for word, with sellers. It's also important for you to know and utilize museums and collectors' clubs, even though they're less accessible than other sources of antiques.

I won't write about antiques per se because there have been hundreds of books published on the subject, most of them specialized. You should read as much as you can about antiques, and study them in museums and the better shops, keeping their quality in mind as a constant ideal. Then one day if you come face to face with one of these ideals at a price you can afford, you're ready to buy it.

While you're waiting for a coup there's no harm in buying semi-antiques and collectibles, both of which are a lot younger than the true antique's one hundred years, and both of which are well represented in most shops. Collectibles are literally what the word implies—anything that's collected, usually by a large number of people. Collectibles can be old or new. For example, Hummel figurines are widely collected. The older ones are more desirable and expensive, but the new ones are also considered collectible. Semi-antiques are nicely crafted old pieces—for instance, anything in the Art Deco style of design—which can be found in antiques shops and shows but aren't old enough to qualify as real antiques. Some people will tell you to buy new merchandise with collectible potentiality. That's okay if you have the money and the genius for spotting future collectibles—and an assured life span of fifty more years. However, this book is only about buying antiques and other old pieces.

One more thing: while I can promise that there's still an abundance of nice old pieces being sold for little money, I won't promise that you'll find gold mines. People are more aware than ever of the value of antiques, and they aren't giving them away. There aren't any buried treasures in thrift shops (they've already been dug up by the volunteers). And though you may make a killing some bright Saturday morning, you probably won't duplicate it for the next ten Saturdays.

2
Where to Buy

It took me a lot of time and hitting and missing to learn about the traffic in antiques, where it comes from, how it moves. There was a whole world out there and I began to explore it. I'll begin with antiques shops because they're the most obvious source of supply; and for too many people, they are the only one. By the end of the chapter, though, you'll know a lot more about where to buy, and for the same amount of money the dealers spend.

Antiques shops. I went to big-city and small-town dealers. I found that prices for similar and identical items varied so much from dealer to dealer, it was confusing. (Naturally there aren't as many identical pieces among antiques as among new merchandise, but there are just enough to show you how confusing prices can be.)

Note well—a dealer can charge what he likes to think the object is worth or what the traffic will bear. There are apparently no governmental or economic restrictions on antique dealers. If you're a tyro collector, you may pay exorbitant prices before you wise up. It takes a bit of expensive practice to learn to bargain and buy effectively. *In the beginning you should browse extensively and buy sparingly at antiques shops, because that's how you'll learn what antiques are and approximately what they should cost.*

Unfortunately for our pocketbooks, some of the finest antiques can only be found in the shops. Once in a great while I feel I have to splurge. If I see something I can almost afford that captures my heart and soul, I grab it while it's hot. I learned the hard way that you have to make up your mind quickly if the item is desirable. . . .

More than ten years ago, on a whim, I entered the small shop of a glass-only dealer. Her display was dazzling, colorful, legitimate, old, much of it hand-blown and really high-priced. I could see it was almost museum quality. How dare I consider buying anything here?

But I have always thrilled to good glass. The kindhearted proprietress, a glass expert, gave me an education during my two visits with her. Meantime I fell in love with a forty-five-dollar yellow Sandwich-glass dolphin candlestick (it's worth much more today). It was cheaper than most of her other pieces because it had a slight flaw. I didn't have enough experience then to try to bargain it down on the basis of its damage.

Well, I agonized over that forty-five dollars. Should I spend that much, and how would I get the money? I must have used up the better part of a week coming to a positive decision about the candlestick. Then I had to scheme up various ways to scrape the money together. It seemed to take forever, and I wasn't sure the little dolphin hadn't been sold. But the day finally came, more than a month later, when I had the money.

I raced all the way to the shop, only to hit a blank wall. The place was closed, bolted, and partially empty. From the next-door neighbor I learned that this vivacious, eloquent, barely middle-aged lady was seriously ill with a totally unsuspected cancer. Believe me when I tell you that I've rarely seen such lovely glass, or felt so sad about a stranger. I never went back, but

I learned for future reference that "he who hesitates is lost."

Garage sales. It was Janet, the friend I mentioned in Chapter 1, who told me about the classified pages. This opened endless doors for me: the classified pages were where I found that particular delight of my heart, the garage sale; and garage sales are where I get bargains in antiques. There are classified pages in every daily newspaper in the United States, as well as in most weeklies. There are even a few all-classified papers. Large suburbs and small towns have the greatest number of advertised garage sales.

If you live in or are visiting a large city, you can find garage sales in the biggest dailies, though they're sometimes camouflaged as "apartment sales" or given other designations. You should also look into the many small daily, weekly, and monthly publications issued for and by civic, social, and political groups, and in geographical subdivisions of the city. The best way to locate these is by looking in the classified (yellow) pages of the phone book under "Publications—Periodicals" or the equivalent. Or speak to the proprietors of different newsstands around the city. They know all the publications worth knowing.

Garage sales offer old, collectible, and antique items at phenomenally low prices, for the most part. But proprietors of garage (basement, yard, lawn, attic, porch, patio) sales aren't charitably motivated. They charge what the traffic will bear. They're entrepreneurs going after the fast buck so they can buy Johnny a bigger bicycle for his birthday. Their items are usually used, their terms, cash, and their profits minimal and negotiable.

Garage sales are everywhere, even as far off as Puerto Rico and Canada. However, most of them are in your own backyard. Once you become aware of and start looking for them, their notices will jump out at you wherever you go. The supermarket bulletin board is one of the most popular posting places. Another favorite spot is the local telephone pole.

The first time I noticed one of the latter, I was behind the wheel waiting for a red light. I looked up and there it was—a pink patch of paper on the nearest pole. I was very excited as I scribbled the information from the tiny flyer (most notices are bigger) onto a loose paper in my bag. I forgot about the traffic light and all the cars behind me.

"Lady! What the hell are you doing?" A strange man was at my window.

I hugged the paper guiltily to my chest and checked the light. It was definitely green.

"I'm sorry, I'll go right now—I'm sorry . . ."

I thought the man was going to slug me. He was one of those red-faced types who always threaten women drivers.

"Get a move on, get a move on!!"

"Yes sir, yes sir . . ." I don't think he expected me to move so fast. His mouth was still open as I blasted off.

I've come to sudden stops in front of at least five hundred telephone poles since then. I've heard other horns and other voices, but I keep doing it. On the basis of personal experience, I'd say the garage-sale notice has become a menace to the road.

Rummage sales. You may not believe it, but rummage prices are lower than those at garage sales. Rummages are usually held by social, civic, and religious institutions (often in their big Bingo hall). They're seasonal, coming before Christmas or Easter, or whenever the church needs money. The merchandise is donated by both charitable and coerced members; there's no rent and little other overhead, thereby guaranteeing the organization a 100 percent profit. Rummage notices are circulated around town much the same as those for garage sales.

I had a frightening introduction to rummage advertising. I was wheeling a shopping cart out of the supermarket one busy Saturday, when I spotted a paper under my left windshield wiper.

"Oh-oh!" I said it out loud, my heart skipping three beats as I recalled my husband's frown the last time I got a ticket for parking.

"They can't give me a ticket in a parking lot!" My blood pressure rose a few degrees as I readied for the fight. I snatched the offending paper off the windshield and quickly saw its true contents. I was boiling inside until I started reading: the local Catholic church was holding a rummage next week, featuring clothes, toys, dishes, glasses, boots and rubbers, books, white elephants (old, old pieces the owners don't want anymore); and, at the very bottom of the page, I noticed they were selling "a few antiques." I totally forgot my pique as I carefully noted, folded, and put away the flyer. That was my first rummage sale, and it fulfilled all its promises. I've been hooked on them ever since.

Unlike the garage sale, the rummage doesn't specialize in hard goods. Used clothes are the biggest, hottest item at a rummage. Sometimes they have very impressive labels in them, and sell for peanuts. The volunteer workers try to keep the merchandise neat and clean. And, of course, there's at least one table of hard goods. Here you can find everything from juice squeezers to ten-cent pieces of old marcasite jewelry.

Bazaars. Next of kin to the rummage is the bazaar, which is generally sponsored by the same organizations as the former. The main difference is that bazaars proudly feature new merchandise. So why do I go? Because more and more bazaars are setting up white-elephant tables and antiques booths. I also go because they have reasonable prices on new clothes and household goods. The stock is sold cheaply because it's been extorted from helpless business people in the name of charity. And so, if you buy cheap new bazaar merchandise (only because you need it), you'll save enough money to treat yourself to an antique.

Just plain folks. This category is my own invention. It consists of friends, relatives, neighbors, and even strangers. These people have heirlooms shoved into dark places because they hate them. They might have thrown them out, but value has a way of perpetuating itself. I had the marvelous luck to buy a few such lovely old pieces from one of my neighbors. (She didn't think they were lovely.) The story of how and where I found these items is unbelievable and will follow later on.

Get busy on the people you know. Open their doors and drawers. Mess up their attics and basements. Some entrepreneurs are able to get rich quick in the attic-cleaning business. But you don't have to go to extremes —just run out and ring bells. Knock knockers at old farmhouses: you'll get your foot in the door or in your mouth, but it's an even chance you'll come up with some cheap antiques.

Auctions. The most variable kinds of goods, including a wide range of antiques, are handled by auctioneers. Some of these sales are conducted for the benefit of institutions. Most are legitimate. This means that starting prices are kept to a minimum, sealed bids are forbidden, and all items are sold, no matter how low the final bid. You can get to know the auctioneers by going to their sales and then following their newspaper ads. You should be able to get wonderful buys.

My husband and I took his parents to a middle-priced auction in an aristocratic old town in the Berkshire mountains of Massachusetts. It was one of those affairs held under a tent filled with hundreds of chairs. That meant there was overhead. Furthermore, the middle-aged ladies wore conservative, no-style dresses, the kind that meant this was a moneyed crowd.

"Remember that nice dresser we gave to the janitor

on East Twenty-third Street, Laura?" My father-in-law had his hand on a termite-ridden plain old pine dresser.

"They're going to *sell* this?" my mother-in-law asked incredulously.

My in-laws recognized a couple of other items they had owned in their less affluent days, and subsequently discarded; a curved glass china closet that sold at the auction for $350 ("You told me to give it to the Salvation Army; it was too small," my father-in-law scolded); and a complete set of pink Depression glass dinnerware, which sold for $110. The dresser, termites and all, went for $530.

"That auctioneer is a crook!" resounded my mother-in-law's final judgment.

Swap and shop. These markets are the craziest of all antiques suppliers. They're large and unwieldy, and you can walk around for hours finding one antique after another or none at all. Swap and Shops spring up like weeds at drive-in theaters, abandoned airplane hangars, racetracks, parking lots, unused fairgrounds, armories, and on and on. Most of them have room for hundreds of cars which you, the buyer or seller, park for a nominal sum of one dollar to more than ten dollars at the largest markets. The car then becomes your shop.

You'll find everything for sale. The sellers are like you, either honest or larcenous. A few are dealers dressed like Little Red Riding Hood's grandmother. Prices are unreal; they're either too much or too little. You have to use your expertise to determine value, and your bargaining ability to bring prices down. And some people really do swap.

Flea markets. These have a more professional aura than Swap and Shop, with dealers and semi-pros paying quite a bit for indoor or outdoor booths. Huckstering is more obvious, and there are almost no raw amateurs behind the counters. Like vagabonds, the flea marketeers carry their packs on their backs and follow the trail wherever it takes them, sometimes hundreds (or thousands) of miles. You expect to get better buys at flea markets than at antiques shops because the overhead is lower. The merchandise is correspondingly less impressive, but I've seen some fine pieces too.

There's another kind of flea market that combines professionals with amateurs, the latter representing some local organization out to raise money for a good cause. You have to be one step ahead of the amateurs on prices because they often don't know what they're doing. I found this especially true at a recent benefit sale for sufferers of a serious illness. I had, as usual, approached the white elephant table with great expectations. What a pleasant surprise to find myself confronted by more genuine antiques than white elephants. Pleasant, that is, until I saw the high prices. I couldn't believe them.

One of the volunteers brought a newly donated Roseville planter (which I immediately wanted) to a managerial-looking woman behind the table. Was it possible?—I saw the woman consult the current *Price Guide to Antiques*, the American antiques dealers' bible. Sure enough, she marked the planter at the antique shop level, looking very smug about her coup.

I walked around the large room, looked things over, and came back like a homing pigeon to the antiques. The same objects were still standing, untouched. Laughing to myself, I went out to some nearby garage sales and returned an hour later. I really wanted the Roseville piece. By this time prices were coming down like Newton's apple, and the merchandising expert's face had fallen with them. I was ready to bargain.

Well, P.S., I got my planter for five dollars less, and the cause still made a good profit.

Thrift shops. These used to be very cheap, but their prices are going up. They're beginning to charge intermediate prices for mediocre antiques. If the dealer gets there early, he takes it all. And sometimes he has a permanent deal with the right people. (In spite of my cynicism, I will admit that you can still get good buys in antiques and fine old furniture.) These shops are usually run by churches and charitable institutions and are often found in otherwise unrentable out-of-the-way stores. Canny and uncanny little old ladies are behind the counters.

The Salvation Army is a category unto itself. It's the biggest name in the thrift business, frequently utilizing a self-owned building for the sale of everything from used appliances and furniture to clothing. Stores are staffed by paid workers and rehabilitated people. Proceeds go to every good cause imaginable.

Country or county fairs are exhibiting antiques more self-consciously than ever before. The antiques were always there, but they used to be called by their real name, second-hand goods, and they went for pennies. The fairs are held in somewhat rural areas (though some are suburban), and have produce, games, competitions, homemades, and rides. Most move around from place to place, except for those that are annual, seasonal, or occur every weekend. In all these operations you'll find more primitives and collectibles than fine antiques. You may also come across sensational buys.

Farmers' markets are more for buying and selling than for games, but they have the flavor of fairs and are often suburban. Their antiques are more or less sophisticated and are housed in individual shops.

Collectors' clubs. You can make personal contacts through these clubs. I've been to some of their meetings, but I don't belong to any one club because I'm a collector of general antiques, not anything as specific as Coca-Cola items, old calendars, dolls (delicious), swords, bottles, or railroadiana. If I had a specific interest I would jump into one of these rapidly burgeoning specialized clubs. On the other hand, it isn't always easy to gain membership if the collectible is so popular that the club is already overcrowded.

You can get more information about clubs by reading antiques journals and magazines, which I suggest you borrow from your library, if possible, because they're expensive. If you're lucky, you'll meet members while you're out buying, and you can ask them questions. True collectors are goldmines of information. They know a lot because they read, correspond, and get together at regular intervals all over the country to compare notes, eat, swap, and buy and sell. They also plan their vacations to correspond with national meetings.

Antiques shows are one of the best places for learning, but you pay for it (the price of admission). Here's how you go about it: try to get around to all the dealers (which number anywhere from fifty to a hundred and fifty), acting like a prospective buyer, examining the merchandise, and admiring it. Every so often, when you come across a really interesting piece, pick the seller's brains with a battery of pertinent questions, making him sweat for the money he thinks you're going to spend on the item. When it's all over, you can tell him you want to look around some more before making up your mind.

The prices of antiques at these shows are higher than what you'll find in the shops. But the quantity is extraordinary. Nowhere else can so much be seen under one roof. It's a marvelous way to get to know prices and pieces, as well as to realize your own net worth.

And I'll personally guarantee that out of all those dealers, you'll find at least one who's cheap enough for you—maybe even two.

Museums. These are one of the most recent sources of supply for antiques at all prices, though most are intermediate. Lately a few museums have been deaccessioning some of their duplicate or less desirable acquisitions, many of which had been stored for generations. They're authentic and fairly priced, and some are even documented. They're sold in the museum shops along with a number of imported antiques. Prices are fixed; you can't bargain. Some museum-owned objects are sold at auction and you can do as well or as badly as you would at an outside auction.

The biggest problem with the museum is its location. Usually it's in or near a city. You may have to travel to get there. But do it because that's where you'll see the beauty of ancient worlds. Some museums are free but aren't open every day, so write for a time schedule beforehand. You can spend hours looking into the sarcophagus of an ancient pharaoh or wandering through rooms from early castles transported stone by stone from Europe. You'll get to see the highest quality artifacts, and you'll be able to study their history.

3
How to Budget

I'm going to give you, the inflation-ridden reader, some marvelous suggestions for saving a bundle of cash through petty economies. You could then deposit this cash in an inaccessible bank account paying eternal interest. And, as it says in the TV commercials, you'd be a quarter of a million dollars richer at age 165.

However, I have other plans for your savings. I'm going to help you spend them on antiques. By following my recommendations, you'll stop eating, drinking, smoking, and enjoying whatever vices you've so carefully acquired and nurtured over the years, and you'll buy antiques instead.

Personally I don't care if my readers never eat again. I'm tired of hearing Mrs. Fat America bemoan her superweight whenever she can capture a bored listener. We're a nation of overeaters, and if you're the culprit who's been bringing home too many potato chips and too much soda—or too much food altogether—*stop now*. That's empty-calorie money you're spending.

You could easily remove five dollars' worth of junk foods from your weekly budget, but I'll settle for two dollars' worth. And figure another two dollars a week on soda, beer, fruit drinks, and the like. This builds up to at least $208 extra per year in your pocket, and it leaves your family free to find constructive alternatives to useless eating.

And how about the size of the portions you lay on the dinner table? I'll bet they're very big. You could be saving another $100 a year (or more after recovering from your withdrawal symptoms) on meat and potatoes alone.

Your next step is to learn how to buy food. It's really simple. First, follow the sales advertised by most markets once a week in your local paper (the one you've already bought for the classified section). Then drive or walk (whichever uses least gas) to the store that has the most sale items for your needs. You'll be able to stock up on toilet paper this week, canned soup next week, detergents and margarine the week after. You'll save about $104 per annum this way—and more, if you barely try. And if you think you're giving out more money than you're getting back, wait. In no time at all, the savings will catch up with the spending and return to you in the form of antiques.

All of the above is predicated on the principle of women's lib. That is, if you're the chief food buyer, it's your civil right to manage the total food budget. In other words, you appropriate a lump sum for yourself every time your husband gets paid. How else are you going to juggle the money?

There are still women living in the dark ages of male financial dominance, whereby the man doles out the money in slow droplets. Either these women liberate themselves, or they forget about buying antiques! I'm reminded especially of the lady I met at a rummage sale, the cheapest form of sale anywhere. I noticed her because she was fondling an old pressed glass vase that appeared to be in perfect condition.

I followed her all over the room hoping she would give up her lovely treasure. After a while she came out of her trance and recognized in me a fellow antiquer. She poured out her heart to me: "Isn't this beautiful?

I love pressed glass. And look—you can see how old it is, probably from the nineteenth century. Three dollars isn't too much; I'd pay ten in a shop—if I had ten. I don't even have three." I thought she was going to cry but she composed herself. "Actually, I have the three dollars but I'm supposed to spend it at the bakery. If I buy this vase, I'll have to tell my husband I have no bread or cake for dinner and he'll hit the ceiling."

I got the picture. She was paid by the day. He knew what she expected to buy and how much each item cost, and he gave her the exact amount within fifty cents.

"How come you're here?"

"Oh, well, sometimes you can get things for a dime or a quarter." She didn't look poor or abused.

"Don't you get a weekly food allowance, with something left over for you?"

"Oh, we never did that. If I need anything, I ask."

"On your hands and knees?" She didn't blow up at me so I got more nervy. "Downtrodden women of the world, unite! You have a steady job; get paid for it. Did you ever hear of women's lib?"

"Well, I—yes—"

"It's time for you to change. Ask him for a reasonable sum every week and cut corners like mad. Stop smoking—no, you're not a smoker," I could see from her rapt expression that I was getting through. "And buy, buy, buy antiques!"

Yes, she bought the vase. My evangelism cost me dear. Her last words to me were, "I'm going to bake a cake and toast some old bread I have." But would she demand a weekly allowance? Anyhow, I'd planted the seed.

Clothing is one of the three major expenditures (food and shelter being the other two). If you like lots of clothes and you'd have a conflict about giving them up for antiques, used clothes are an ideal solution. For a long time I couldn't imagine myself in somebody else's castoffs. Then one day a while back, I stopped at one of my favorite out-of-the-way suburban thrift shops to browse. As I was opening the door my eyes were caught by a window display of one of the smartest skirt suits I'd ever seen. I was steeling myself against its blandishments when I caught sight of the highly visible inside label—Neiman-Marcus of Texas!

I had never owned and could never hope to own an original like this. I was weakening. I succumbed when I saw the size (mine) and the price, $2.50 (prices have risen with inflation). I wondered vaguely why no one had grabbed it.

"Can I try on that suit? The one in the window I mean—would you mind?"

"Oh, no—impossible. We just dressed the window and it doesn't get changed for a whole week," explained the lady behind the counter.

A second lady reminded her that "that other woman put a dollar deposit on the suit."

"But you can second reserve it in case she doesn't want it."

I paid my dollar and spent the rest of the week in mounting suspense—over used clothes. How unbelievable! To make an anxious story short, I got lucky. The suit didn't fit her at all, but it was great for me. I bought it. Every time I wore it I got compliments. I was hooked forever. Now I go to rummage sales in affluent communities or I buy couturier styles in affordable thrift shops. Wearing used clothes is probably safer (after cleaning) than eating from antique dishes that may have dispensed tainted foods.

You can also save money by not buying fad clothing. Kooky shoes, see-through shirts, and ragged blue jeans are for your kids, not for you. Kids have to look like their peers, or they feel traumatized. But here's what happens to their mothers who run out and buy all the new juvenile clothing fads:

One of my neighbors slavishly imitates her daughter's apparel. I have a hard time distinguishing between them because their height and build are almost identical, their hair color comes out of the same bottle, and the hair swings onto both pairs of shoulders with the same jaunty abandon.

One day as I was watering my plants—which allows me a panoramic view of neighborhood secrets—I observed the mother step off the curb to cross the street. Creeping up behind her was a tall boy whom I recognized as one of her daughter's teen-age friends. Suddenly he darted forward and locked his arm around her waist. This could have been discounted by the woman as mistaken identity, except that at the same time he cupped his hand over her breast and squeezed for all the world to see.

"What are you doing!!" she screeched.

I'll always remember the funny look of horror on that boy's face as he recognized his mistake. To compound his anguish, the daughter came running out of the house to greet him. That set off a tornado.

"Do you let him do this to you? Answer me!!"

I moved away from the window so I could laugh without being seen. I wondered whether she would punish her daughter or change her own style of dress. The latter would certainly save everybody's nerves and a few bucks, I thought. She never took my silent advice.

I realize that clothing money doesn't come out of your personal budget, as food does. I therefore can't give you a reckoning in dollars and cents to add to the previous sums saved. But if you buy good used clothes and take advantage of end-of-season sales (see ahead), you'll save plenty. You're entitled to a few antiques after all that.

Shelter is the third big budget category. Unfortunately it can't figure into your own personal yearly savings. If you're an established homeowner, you're in a set financial pattern, and that's that. But if you're about to buy a house, I have one crucial money-saving recommendation: shop around carefully and utilize the free services of every possible real estate office and government agency in your quest for help and information. Too many people put too much income into the family domicile. You'll find yourself in the same bind if you rush or if you buy ignorantly.

Now we come to the nagging etceteras of daily spending. Can you give up cigarettes, hairdressers, impulse buying, coffee shop lunches, unnecessary entertainment, expensive gifts, etcetera? (SCREAM) I deliberately left out the word "antiques" from this list because in a financial sense, antiques aren't an etcetera. They're like a solid 7½ percent investment which rises every year and incidentally gives aesthetic satisfaction.

Let's begin your self-flagellation with cigarettes. If you're a smoker, you can save a lot of money—at least $200 a year for the average smoker—by not buying cigarettes. As an added bonus, you may even save your life. (I'm not going to tell you how to kick the habit. For that, see your local branch of the American Cancer Society.)

You can cut down on visits to the hairdresser by studying your own teenager (female or male), or somebody else's. Today's youngsters go to the haircutters (unisex) only for cuttings and shapings. There they learn to blow-dry and style their own hair with the marvelous electric blowers. If you buy one, follow appliance instructions and use a hair conditioner; you'll save more than fifty dollars a year—much more.

If you work and eat out you're probably putting hundreds of dollars annually into coffee shop lunches. (Even if you don't work you've got to be spending money at places like McDonald's.) As often as possible, prepare a simple sandwich for yourself in the morning. Take it to work or wherever you go. You can still treat yourself and the kids occasionally, while saving at least seventy-five dollars annually.

And how about impulse buying in the supermarket and elsewhere? You don't use half of these purchases, yet I'll bet you spend fifty dollars a year on them. If you're naively wondering, "What does she mean by impulse buying?" let me give you the example of a recently deceased old lady whose estate sale I attended.

I had inspected the whole house and everything in it, but without the usual thrill I feel when I find a cheap antique in one room or another. All I could find to buy were stockings. At a quarter a pair you don't turn them down, but the house was filled with packages and boxes of brand-new stockings.

"This place looks like a department store," I observed to a lady who said she lived in the house next door.

"She liked to buy them."

"Was she worried she'd run out?"

"She just kept buying—and buying, as if she never had enough." The neighbor smiled nostalgically.

And that's what impulse buying is all about. It's a desire to buy and buy. The biggest damage is done during sales, like the January white sales, the Columbus and Election Day sales, the anniversary and end-of-season sales. As I mentioned previously, this is a great time to save money on clothes, but not by buying two of everything because they're cheap and you're on a charge card, "so what the hell!" Wear blinders when you shop so you won't see anything but what you came for. *Then* notice how easily you can coax a few extra dollars out of the family budget for an occasional antique.

Now we come to the grand total of the savings listed throughout this chapter. If you add up all the figures, you'll have $787, or $587, if you didn't smoke to begin with. Either way, that's the bundle I promised you at the beginning. It will buy a lot of cheap antiques, and a few expensive ones you've acquired cheaply. Remember, this is your money from the budgets under your personal management. You'll have to pinch and hustle for it, so you're entitled to invest in antiques.

I still have two etceteras to deal with: expensive

gifts and expensive entertainment. These won't affect your personal budget, but judiciously approached, they can add to the general family savings. Cheap antiques make delightful gifts, with nobody the wiser in terms of what you spent—if you keep your mouth shut. First read this book and practice on yourself. For friends and relatives who scorn antiques, you can also buy brand-new cheap gifts at bazaars and flea markets. Both categories are great for any occasion except those that call for checks. Sorry about that.

Expensive entertainment can also be cut considerably. Shop around for cheap movies. If you can't afford big-time shows, concerts, lectures, and cultural exhibits, take advantage of the free or inexpensive offerings by local governments, schools and universities, libraries, museums, and art galleries. They're listed in your newspapers. Even auctions count as entertainment.

One last word on buying used goods. I don't recommend the purchase of used cars or large appliances through the classifieds. Let the buyer beware, even if the ad swears the product was used only one week by a little old lady who cashed in her chips. You don't get warranties or guarantees, as in new items. You might buy something that's doctored to look good today, only to break down tomorrow. (I just wanted to go on record with that; now you can do as you please.)

On the other hand, I'm all for buying small appliances used. By a small appliance I mean anything you can pick up with one hand. You can usually buy them cheaply and in good condition at garage sales. But make sure there's an electric outlet in the garage so you can test the appliance. (You can also get brand-new small appliances at these sales for half price.)

One of my greatest second-hand investments was an old upright vacuum cleaner that did a better job on high shag carpeting than the new one I had just bought and regretted purchasing. The old vacuum cleaner was sitting in the middle of a garage sale, tagged at three dollars. I was tempted.

"What's wrong with it?" I asked the proprietress.

"It runs, it runs! Here, plug it in; try it!"

It ran.

"Will you take two dollars?" fell out of me automatically.

"Sure!" Was it my imagination or was she too willing?

I found out when I got home. The machine vacuumed the shag beautifully until the motor started to smoke.

I patronize an inexpensive reliable repair shop in the neighborhood. They charged $18.75 to fix the machine. The mechanic made a special point of coming out to tell me how marvelous these old metal vacuum cleaners are, and how many commercial enterprises are buying them up and getting them refurbished. (If you send me a postcard, I'll tell you the brand name and approximate year.)

I'll discuss used furniture at length in the thrift shop and garage sale chapters. In a few words, I believe in used furniture, the kind that was made at a time when craftsmanship was high and quality enduring. You'd have to pay a fortune for its equivalent today. So try to track down used and antique furniture pieces. They're available at reasonable prices. But if you must have new merchandise, *buy on sale*. Sooner or later, every furniture store has a sale. Big department stores also sell from their warehouses. And if you intersperse the modern with the antique, the effect is fabulous.

Good luck!

4
Antiques Shops

Once upon a time I cherished a kind of gingerbread stereotype of the typical antiques shop. It was called "Grandma's Attic," and was filled with neatly-stacked, well-scrubbed charming old pieces of china and glass that got feather dusted every day by a sweet, befuddled, frail proprietress named Grandma. Up to then I don't think I had ever walked into an antique shop in my life.

Now I have. But the proprietors are varied and not one of them has resembled my archetypal grandma. I've found plenty of "Grandma's Attics" though. I've also found dozens of other names that repeat themselves everywhere I go. See if you recognize a few: "Trash and Treasure," "Picket Fence," "Ye Olde Curiosity Shoppe," "Red Barn," "Red Shed," "Spinning Wheel," "Wagon Wheel," "Gift Horse," "Past and Present," "Time Was," "Yesterday and Today," "Now and Then," "Thieves' Den," "Cracker Barrel," "Golden Oldies," "Lavender and Lace," "Antiques and Junktiques," "Lamp Post," "Trading Post," and on and on. Many stores carry the first name of the owner (who is usually a woman) followed by various euphemisms for the word store, including "Shoppe," "Emporium," "Exchange," "Gallery," "Antiques," "Pavilion," "Interiors," "Corner," and "Cottage."

The people who run these stores-with-similar-names are both stereotyped and unique, much like their merchandise. You distinctly recognize both the human and inanimate objects, yet you've never seen an exact duplicate of either. My own carefully nourished grandma stereotype was partially destroyed the day I entered a real gingerbread house of so-called antiques. I had driven past the place a number of times, and was fascinated by its promising exterior. I finally weakened, parked, and entered. I was left to myself to browse among the unrelieved junk merchandise (what a disappointment!) for fully five minutes. The dusty, dreary interior climate was getting to me when its octogenarian owner entered. She was easily the oldest antique in the place, and not at all like my imaginary grandma. I was wondering how I could duck past this hungry-looking ferret-faced madam without buying anything, when I saw the knife in her hand. I almost jumped out of my skin. It was no artifact, nor was it a simple paring knife or letter opener. It was the kind butchers use to trim whole sides of beef.

Suddenly this shriveled-up old lady appeared demented to me—crazy enough to plunge her knife into an unsuspecting customer in a musty house that nobody else had entered for what might have been years. Would my body be found? She had laid her trap carefully, letting me explore at will (most antiques shop proprietors are casually vigilant), waiting for me to drop my guard, penetrate to the inner rooms—and whammo! what a way to go. . . .

I looked around frantically for a cheap, not too ugly memento, the purchase of which might divert her from her evil plans. I grabbed up a piece of something and flung it in front of her like a sacrifice: "I want that!" Now, for the first time, she released the knife. I watched it in fascination. She was busy bagging the purchase and making change as I backed out. She happened to mention that store owners couldn't be too careful these days, what with burglars and muggers. It was only when I made my escape that I wondered whether the whole thing was a ploy to trick people into buying her shoddy merchandise. I never found out.

Most dealers are more subtle than my grandma-with-the-knife. You have to play a different kind of game with them. Bear in mind that when you buy at an antiques shop, *you're working as much with dealer personality as with product.* Remember this when it's time to bargain over a price. (Bargaining is an accepted procedure in antiques shops.) You should learn to be a psychologist if you want to buy antiques cheaply. Also you have to be a poker player, a diplomat, a con artist, and a student of the human soul. To gain the upper hand, get to know the various types you'll be dealing with. Here's a general outline:

There are more women than men in the business, although the fine shops on the best avenues in the biggest cities are generally run by men (smooth, sophisticated, executive types). These uptown smoothies more or less intimidate me. I haven't the thousands of dollars needed even to say hello to them. From time to time I've mustered the nerve to squeeze through their doors unobtrusively and pretend I'm interested in a piece that almost looks cheap. I never stay long, although I could because nobody bothers to look at me. They know.

There are also owners of secondhand furniture businesses who have drifted into antiques. They know their merchandise as well as the more expensive entrepreneurs. And there are furniture warehouse owners and real estate brokers who dabble in antiques. All of them know their merchandise well.

But by and large, it's a ladies' business. The women get started by collecting themselves right out of their homes. For the older generation it seems like a natural female calling, and you see more middle-aged women than young ones. Some form partnerships, and others work with their husbands.

There are a few younger women too. I used to visit a store whose proprietress wore miniskirts and low-cut blouses. At the other extreme were two glamorous young ladies who regularly wore evening skirts. Both types intimidate me. I feel much more at home with that ubiquitous antiques-dealer prototype, the fat lady in the dirty smock and torn house slippers. Her love for her stock is the only aesthetic in her life. Occasionally, as a gesture to her calling, she'll wear a magnificently jeweled Georgian brooch against a stained housedress.

In the ma-and-pa shops the woman is more the owner, a queen bee with her drone standing by to do the heavy moving. I know one such couple very well. She always looks and sounds angry (she's an ex-alcoholic who was probably sweeter when drunk). He's her whipping boy, and the customers know it. But they keep going back in spite of the unpleasant atmosphere because they find an unlimited supply of antiques that are usually cheap.

You'll also see very young couples trading in antiques. They have the strength and know-how to strip and refinish furniture. They work harmoniously in out-of-the-way cheaply rented stores or at flea markets or in communes along country roadsides in the summer.

So now you've visited a few antiques shops run by a few of the above dealers, and you've finally found a piece you must have more than anything else in the world (but don't gasp with excitement; it sends the price up). The next step is to woo the dealer in order to get the best possible buy. Her prices are more flexible than new-item prices but she naturally wants to make a top profit. Analyze her. Be friendly. If her personality overwhelms you or if it's difficult for you to create a superficial relationship, let *her* make the over-

Antiques Shops

tures. She wants you as a customer so she'll try her best to be nice, to be accommodating, to be helpful, to make you feel relaxed. As you buy more you'll see I'm right: it's a personality market, and if you work it artfully you can bring prices down to a more negotiable level.

A business that depends so much on individual personality can have unexpected pitfalls. Be prepared for occasional disappointments like the one I had a few summers ago on my vacation. I had found a splendid barn bristling with lovely pieces of small old furniture —footstools, spinning wheels, planters, wicker oddities, tables—all easily transportable and in good condition. I fell in love with a footstool and a yarnwinder but I couldn't find anyone to sell them to me.

The next time I visited the barn, full of desire, I saw a plainly-dressed woman with stern, introspective features, trailed by several prospective buyers. She must be the one! I tried to catch her so I could give her my best getting-to-know-you routine, but she was as elusive as a bird. Why couldn't she be pinned down?

I decided to try once more. The next day I was able to collar the lady, and started with my infallible weather routine: "What a sticky day—" Her impassive eyes told me my verbal cliches would have to go, and the rest of my bargaining formula too.

"How much is the yarnwinder?" I almost screamed. I had to hold onto her.

"Thirty-five dollars." My expression must have told her it was too much because she started to walk away. Maybe the footstool would be cheaper.

"And the footstool—the footstool?—that one!"

Her eyes followed my finger. "That one? It's t-t-t-t-t-t-t-t-" Two dollars? Ten? Twenty? She couldn't jump the hurdle of that "t." She was a stutterer! No wonder she didn't want to talk.

We looked at each other in momentary silence. As much as I wanted the footstool, I couldn't force her through the same ordeal again. Almost all the other pieces were marked but I didn't want them. What was to be done?

Nothing. I couldn't even have softened her up with conversation. In a case like this either pay the price or be prepared for disappointment.

I've talked about bargaining throughout this chapter. Now I want to tell you how to do it, step by step. It's a cat-and-mouse game more ancient than the product you're haggling over. You'll become more proficient each time you do it. I think you'll feel more comfortable if you're aware that most dealers expect you to bargain. Some will tell you early in the game that they're a one-price store. On the other hand, I know a dealer who instructs her assistant (in front of the customers) that certain pieces can come down 10 percent, others 15 percent, and still others, 20 percent. There's almost always a large markup on antiques; you should try to negotiate price with all the sellers.

Here's how you get started:

1. Always stay calm, cool, and collected.
2. Don't show you're interested in a specific piece.
3. Ask the prices of three or four pieces, including the one you like.
4. If the prices are already marked, you can eliminate step three.
5. Hold two pieces (the one you want and one you don't want) and mull over them for a while. Never rush into the sale.
6. Finally, put the two pieces on the counter and ask—with simulated confidence—if she can give you a "somewhat better price." Ask in your most ladylike tone, not the one you use on the butcher.
7. If she says no, put the pieces back and slowly leave. More often than not she's playing a game, in which case you'll get a better price just as you reach the door.

8. But she'll probably say yes, and give you 10 to 20 percent off.
9. Don't expect a markdown on a cheap item unless you buy several things.
10. While you're paying your money pick her brain. Find out everything you can about your purchase and its entire genre. Dealers can be your best source of information if you don't read or go to museums (you should do both). Some are bursting with knowledge about their specialties, others know a little about a lot, and still others have educated themselves through the years and are willing to educate the customer. There's nothing like money to break the ice and further your education. You two will have become bosom buddies by the time the last penny has been counted.

The stock is more important than personalities and bargaining in the average antiques shop. "Average" is the moderately priced neighborhood store that carries everything. This is the place that will become most familiar to you. If you're reading this book you're not a potential habitué of the four- and five-figure big-city gallery. Neither will you get to the wholesale houses. Or Europe. Or Japan.

Most stores have a bit of everything, but some won't touch furniture or jewelry or various specialities, such as dolls. Get to know stock and prices from store to store, even if you have to travel a bit. Browse. You'll be encouraged to do so by the owners. And take your time. You'll soon observe that certain shops charge more or less than the average for similar pieces. One place will deal only in top quality merchandise. Another will have cheaper stuff. Some dealers cram their shelves indiscriminately, which is great if you're missing pieces and parts and want to fill in. Yet another dealer will offer to find whatever you want or need, at a price. Antiques is a many-faceted business.

Here and there, a few dealers do specialize. A highly specialized shop is one that exhibits a large quantity of one type of antique over all others, for instance, Victorian furniture, or art glass, or old jewelry, or lighting fixtures. The dealer will charge a lot of money for individual items within his specialty because he knows he can offer you a wider choice than anyone else. Conversely, he'll be lax about pricing pieces he doesn't care about but which he accumulated as part of his general stock.

I stumbled into a marvelous glass collection in the farm home of a doddering local postmistress in rural Maine. It was a general antiques shop, but glass was its fabulous main line. I rubbed my hands in glee and thought, here's where I get the buy of the century! I was surrounded by glass of every period, color, and variety. There wasn't a price in sight and I was too naive at that time to know the danger signs. I poked and picked for half an hour and came up with five choice pieces for pricing.

"Oh, that's gay nineties; it's thirty-five dollars. That's a Sandwich vase—fifty-five. The miniature Sandwich lamp is a hundred seventy—"

"That much!" I blurted before she could finish.

Fast as a frog's tongue, she whisked two price guides from under her counter. "I'll show you *higher* prices. Right on this page it says . . ."

I didn't hear another word. My innocent little grandma was a shrewd horse trader with the power of the printed page to back her up.

Sadly I returned my choices to their shelves. I hated to leave empty-handed but I wasn't budgeted for this kind of costly merchandise. The most adroit bargaining wouldn't have helped.

I was on my way out, still looking hungrily into every corner, when my eye was drawn to a small, charming, original primitive oil painting propped carelessly on the floor. I grabbed it up.

"How much is this?" I demanded, tossing all my bargaining rules to the wind.

She barely gave it a side glance. "That?" She thought for a minute. "Ten dollars." She didn't look at it again. I figured it was worth five times as much, so I paid without a word and walked slowly out of the house. I didn't have to run. I already knew as a result of this visit that a shop of good old Sandwich glass didn't specialize in primitive paintings from nearby farmhouses. And that's what I mean when I say dealers are lax about pricing outside their specialties.

Before I leave the general subject of stock, or merchandise, I want to warn you that not everything you see in the antiques store is antique, or even old. There are and always have been marvelous reproductions flooding the antiques market. An honest dealer will tell you which is which. But she may be unwittingly buying and selling reproductions. A dishonest dealer will deliberately sell new for old. You'll have to rely on your own knowledge and judgment to distinguish between the two. You get smart only after you've made enough mistakes, after you've done enough buying, and after you've heard enough lies.

I wish I could give you a foolproof way to determine age. There are whole books written on the subject. You're told, for instance, to watch for patina, which is a mellowed look that an object acquires when it gets old enough. Old furniture looks richer than the new product. Old glass is less shiny. Sometimes a chip or crack or fading is a sign of age, although the purists won't touch a piece that's less than perfect. I love antiques because they are old, feel old, look old, and have a long, unknown history behind them. Maybe you just have to sense age. You'll know the signs after a while and still you'll get fooled, because the manufacturers make such clever imitations.

Japan, Hong Kong, and Taiwan are reproducing American antiques. China is reproducing its own antiques, as is Japan. Some of the import labels carry occidental business names. If you don't spend a lot of money on your mistakes, you won't feel so bad. So keep the costs down. That's what this book is all about.

For quality, cheapness, and a wide selection, you may do best in the so-called "concession" antiques shops. This is a whole new category for you to look into. The term concession indicates that the merchandise is borrowed, leased, rented, or bought from a parent company. Carvel's and McDonald's are concessions. Concession antiques shops are run by proprietors who display merchandise loaned by absentee owners, and who take a percentage of each sale. In this way heirlooms leave their homes for the first time and are put on the open market. The owner sets the price, which is non-negotiable, because he's not around to bargain with.

There's something you should be aware of: anybody can bring anything into a concession shop. You'll find therefore that dealers who can't unload their dogs in their own stores give them over to concessionaires. You have to know prices and merchandise well in order to pick up bargains.

Two of the best possible times to patronize antiques shops is either when they're having a grand opening or are closing for good. They'll advertise for either occasion, offering their wares at sharply reduced prices. I followed the activities of two young women who hammered and sawed a very old store into shape for displaying antiques. When the shop opened it had a certain charisma, but not enough to keep going. In order to drum up business they almost had to give away their merchandise. I did very well there, and so did all the other first-week customers.

You can call this a very short story, because when I went back to the store six months later it was about to close. Most antiques shops take a little longer to fail. But the script here read like a soap opera, with both women tangled up in marriage, divorce, and

Antiques Shops

child custody. They had no time to work at the business. I went there in response to a newspaper ad offering the entire inventory at half price. Some closings are less dramatic, with only a part of the inventory offered at a smaller discount. But opening or closing, the buyer always gets a break.

Another big sale time is just before summer vacation, when stores close for a specified period. But you have to watch out for what's on sale and what isn't. Don't be fooled into thinking that absolutely everything has been marked down. If there's no large, all-inclusive store sign containing precise information, look for markdowns on each ticket. *Don't be afraid to ask for the reduction.* You may not get the piece you want if the sale is limited. In that case have the owner show you exactly which items are going for less money.

This last section is different from all the others. It is not a "how-to" guide on buying in antiques shops; it's more important. It tells you where the dealers buy so that you can use their sources of supply for your own buying.

Note well: I'm not advising you to bypass the shops altogether, or I wouldn't have bothered to give you the preceding information. Dealers have sources open to them that you can't touch. Some of the oldest and nicest pieces come to them just because they're dealers. Here are a few of the buying methods they use that you can't:

1. They buy whole households for the sake of a few valuable items.
2. They advertise in the papers or in their windows, "BUY AND SELL ANTIQUES."
3. Some dealers are known and easily accessible in a neighborhood. People in need of ready cash bring them their old family treasures. (I know a dealer in a popular mountain resort who cleans up at Christmas. The residents exchange their

heirloom jewelry for just enough cash to buy presents. Come summer, that same jewelry is fetching astronomical prices from eager antiques-minded tourists who wouldn't consider it a vacation without a few indulgences.)
4. Dealers often buy antiques from large companies that sell antiques wholesale to dealers only. These outlets aren't available to the general public.

The next few sources of supply are open to everybody. Here's where you come in. You'll need practice in order to build up expertise. I'm confident you'll do well in all these areas if you keep trying:

1. Like the dealers, you have a right to ring bells and talk to strangers for leads on antiques. You have to get as far away from the big cities as possible, preferably to rural areas where prices haven't skyrocketed—yet. The antiques are there if you're aggressive enough to find them. Always let the owner set the price. If he needs help, remember that there are very few hicks left in rural America, so don't try to cheat.
2. One of the best dealer sources is the auction. Yes, the same auctions you and I have a right to go to. They're advertised in your local papers. The better ones are listed in the back of the Sunday *New York Times*, which has ads from all over the country. And you'd better believe that prices at cheap auctions, except those on the most hotly contested items, are much cheaper than those in the stores. Just follow the bidding of the professionals. They know the retail price. They will stop short when they see their profit will dissipate. That's where you can afford to step in and still get a bargain.
3. You'll also find dealers at garage and rummage sales and at thrift shops—and why not? every-

thing is cheap. There are three separate chapters in this book telling you how to buy in each of these categories. Two words of warning: dealers get to garage and rummage sales before anyone else, and they're adept at grabbing the best stuff first. You have to beat them at their own game. Secondly, sometimes there's collusion between dealers and some paid employees of large thrift shops. I personally witnessed a bottle of gin being passed sub rosa from a man who had previously been identified for me as a dealer, to a woman in charge of the local Salvation Army store. I don't recommend this method to you; it's too expensive. Also, the dealer followed up his gift with a kiss on the hand. That may not be your style. You should be able to find a few legitimate thrift shops, including the Salvation Army's.

4. Finally, a word about shows and exhibits. These too are sources for the dealers, especially those who get in early and grab up the cheapest offerings. Antiques shows have mushroomed into a big industry in the past few years. The American public has grown more and more antiques conscious, and demand for them is burgeoning. For the most part, prices are high. But here and there you'll find marvelous buys at booths that have been set up by dealers or semiprofessionals from remote, inexpensive areas. You have to be able to cover between 50 and 100 booths in order to run down the cheap ones. And you may have to wear out your track shoes to beat the pros.

I'm sure you'll realize dollars-and-cents benefits if you follow my dealer advice. To get the best breaks in the shops, you have to do a lot of studying and only a little buying at first. You can step up the buying after you've been around: there's no substitute for experience.

5
Garage Sales

Garage sales are becoming a booming industry in the United States. Any amateur can participate because there are no ground rules, no applicable fair trading laws, no sales taxes, no real estate zonings, and no licensing restrictions, except in a very few areas where the frequency of these sales makes temporary licensing lucrative.

I don't need a diploma in garage sales to know why they're so big. Inflation is one of the main reasons. Whereas once upon a time only poor people bought second-hand clothes and goods, now everybody's doing it, and considering himself "in," to boot. The public is finding garage sale items a lot cheaper than brand new balloon-priced department store products.

"Well, I don't buy at garage sales," you insist. You're living in a big-city apartment building with a hundred other families and few garages. You don't even own a car. On the other hand, you have thrift stores all over the city selling second-hand goods cheap, and these may be considered a form of garage sale. Another form is the apartment or merchandise sale advertised in big-city dailies and in some of the other publications I will mention in another section of this chapter. If you live in one of the new condominium apartment complexes you'll find these ads in the publications issued for tenants, and on your lobby bulletin boards.

I don't know how long people have been going to and running garage sales. I remember going to them back in the early 1960s, and before that they probably had a different name. Used goods of all descriptions, including cars and houses, have been advertised since the invention of the printing press. People have worn hand-me-downs as long as they've had clothes on their backs. Swapping—the exchange of goods and services for their equivalents—is another ancient tradition. And finally we have the time-honored antiques business, a highly respectable and lucrative trade in old merchandise.

So what's new about garage sales?

Nothing, except that they're bigger and better than ever. Garage sales are advertised everywhere—in newspapers, bulletins, supermarkets, on telephone poles, and by word of mouth. They're usually held in garages, hence the name. Some people are too lazy to drag the merchandise out of the attic or basement so the sale is given either of those names. The variations are endless.

Here are a few rules of thumb you ought to know if you want to buy successfully at garage sales:

Arrive before the stipulated time of sale. Nothing else is as essential as this. Usually the opening and closing times are given in the announcement. If it says 10 A.M. to 5 P.M., I suggest you be there by 9:30 A.M., or even earlier. Often you'll be allowed to go right in. Other people are also getting in (some buyers go there the day before). By the time the sale begins, the most desirable pieces may be gone. (You too can try going there the day before. You may be allowed to look and buy, or you may not. You may find everything displayed; you may not.) Time is of the essence. You'll get tired of hearing me say this.

I learned about punctuality the hard way. And being dilatory by nature, I had to learn it many times. One of my most painful experiences came early in my antiques career. It was the result of a simple conflict of interest: that is to say, there were two wonderfully appealing sales going on at the same time, on the same day, and I couldn't make up my mind which to go to first.

One of these sales was in a Catholic school where I'd bought an antique majolica plate for thirty-five cents the preceding spring. The other was advertised in these ecstasy-provoking terms:

OLD VICTORIAN HOUSE
Entire contents of grandmother's home, nothing withheld; 60-year accumulation, 5¢ to $25.00; 10 A.M.–5 P.M. Sat. [address].

I woke on the crucial morning still feeling indecisive. And because I was casual about time, I used up a lot of it trying to determine where to go. Well, since the Victorian house was nearer, I thought I'd drop by there and then make up my mind.

I drove happily to my destination, and arrived at five minutes of ten expecting to find a long line outside, which I did. I was glad to see the gingerbread exterior of the house. Older homes always look promising, especially if they're rundown. I parked two blocks away and walked to the line without getting on it (I was that lackadaisical). Meanwhile the starting hour came and went. Rumors were flying: the owners lived upstate and were delayed; nobody was coming; the date had been changed; and so on. People got off the line, and new people got on. And the minutes ticked on.

I didn't know whether the house ad was a hoax or whether the treasures of Croesus stood inside. But I did remember the nice things I'd bought at the school, along with the majolica plate. So without another thought for the lateness of the hour, I went back to my car and was at the school within ten minutes.

The large gym was flooded with people who had known since early morning where they were going. One of them was carrying the usual carnival piece; another had a handsome painting; and there was quite a lot of old glass. But none of it came my way. I was happy to be able to dig a twenty-five-cent pair of mother-of-pearl earrings from a tangled pile of jewelry.

I kept following the people with the treasures, stealing glances at the cheap prices (groan!) and hoping they would let go. Not a chance. Everyone bought what they carried.

"I'll go back to the house!" What a brilliant idea. Maybe the doors were still closed.

My heart was heavy on that seven-minute return trip (I was speeding all the way). Why hadn't I gone to the school first? I was even sorrier when I reached the front of the house and saw people dragging lovely old furniture through the front door, some of it in need of stripping, but no matter. The parade was endless. Furniture, dishes, glass, planters, little things I could only imagine by the gratified expressions on the purchasers' faces.

I didn't go in. Garage sales move very fast. If the prices are right, the place gets dismantled within half an hour, and what's left, I don't want. The prices here must have been supremely right, judging by the flight of the locusts. This was the beginning of my Great Change, and I've been single-minded and almost punctual ever since (often getting there the day before). Really.

Publications. Newspapers are where you'll find most garage sales advertised. Even the largest papers carry ads for them. If the wording doesn't specify "Garage Sale," look under different rubrics, such as "Merchandise for Sale," "Buy and Sell," or "Used Goods." A

Garage Sales

garage sale, by definition, or rather by general understanding, is an exchange of any kind of used merchandise for as little money as possible, usually at the home of the seller, where the general public has been invited. This covers a big chunk of the classifieds under the "Shopping Guide" in your daily paper.

There's an endless variety of publications open to you. The small-town weekly is a great source. If you live in an area in which weekly classified-only papers are published, you can go crazy with pleasure looking through twenty or thirty pages of detailed ads. Most of these notices are for single (or several) items under specific categories, whereas a garage sale is all-inclusive. There are also house organs with classified sections, put out by institutions and businesses. And don't forget trade papers.

If you still don't know which papers to consult for these sales, ask your news vendor. He has many kinds of papers—dailies, weeklies, trade journals, out-of-town, specialized—and knows a little bit about all of them. If you speak a second language, there's got to be a paper in that language, somewhere. It's an education looking for the right publication.

Analyzing the classifieds. Learn how to analyze ads so you won't waste your time going to the wrong garage sales. To me, the most exciting ad is the one that offers "Contents of Old Home," or "Estate Sale" (this last to settle the venerable property of what we hope is an ancient corpse), or "Moving to Florida—everything goes!" In all these ads the whole house is being cleaned out, whereas many garage sales offer only items the seller doesn't want or can't stand anymore.

One year when my husband had to go to Massachusetts on business, we flew in and landed in an area near New Hampshire. I bought the local New Hampshire newspapers (Massachusetts is expensive on antiques) and studied the garage sales. The one that played on my heartstrings started like this: "We Cleaned Out an Old Barn . . . ," and continued in the same vein.

Need I say more? I had rarely seen an ad worded as beautifully and promisingly as that. And it fulfilled my dreams. I found a sterling silver Art Nouveau ring set with a freshwater pearl, and a faintly cracked 1909 calendar plate, each for fifty cents, a marcasite and carnelian pin for seventy-five cents ("That's an antique," the seller said, "we have to charge more for it!"), and various nineteenth-century books all priced under fifty cents apiece.

Remember that you're looking for *cheap* antiques and let this determine your analysis. Wording and length, dates, hours, and merchandise can all be important to ads. You'll learn how to sort them out after you've read a few hundred or so. You may even learn to shun the word antiques. No matter how often you see it, watch out. People have caught on that antiques are in demand and they're hauling out every battered old artifact they own and asking prices that would make a dealer blush. Garage salers who charge antique-store prices are greedy. They don't have the overhead or the wear and tear of a professional; hence they aren't entitled to the same return.

You might look for a simply worded, factual statement that a sale is being conducted at a certain place. Household goods, garden tools, furniture, and the like, are being sold at reasonable prices. More often than not, a few antiques are included, which the owner sees merely as old pieces he doesn't want anymore. Antiques can also be found under such headings as "Musical Instruments," "Pool Tables," "Jewelry," "Games," and that marvelous single word, "Moving."

The garage sale is everywhere. On a warm day in the suburbs, people find garage sale notices growing on trees. They are also found in store windows and on

Garage Sales

supermarket bulletin boards. Probably the suburbs are the most prolific progenitors of these sales. But they're everywhere else too, in all fifty states, Puerto Rico, Canada, and Bermuda.

A couple of years ago my family and I flew down to Puerto Rico for an August vacation. We did it the cheap way (as usual), renting a one-bedroom condominium apartment with a kitchen, which meant I had to prepare a few meals.

As soon as we were unpacked, we set out for the nearest grocery. Since this was my first visit to the Caribbean I naturally expected exotic surroundings, palm trees, lush tropical vegetation, dark-skinned people who spoke only Spanish, pineapples and bananas, and haciendas. Imagine the familiar shock of finding a Grand Union supermarket instead!

I won't discuss Breakstone's cottage cheese and Kellogg's corn flakes. But the added recognition of a bulletin board at the exit door—advertising garage sales!—was beyond my wildest dreams.

"Okay," I announced to my unsuspecting family, "we're in business."

"What are you talking about?" My husband was already annoyed at having to go shopping.

"There's a garage sale tomorrow."

"No! You're on vacation!"

"Oh no, mommy—I wanna swim . . ."

We compromised. I was allowed one sale, with no complaints from anybody. That afternoon we rented a Volkswagen. The next morning we were on our way to the sale.

It wasn't easy following travel directions in our broken Spanish and their broken English (bless my daughter Norma's elementary school for having taught Spanish in the fifth grade). But we finally made it to the sale, where I fell in love with an old hand-carved wooden Santo, the kind that costs so much in the antiques shops. I had picked this small religious statue out of—wouldn't you know it!—the usual welter of odd dishes and glasses, used toys, and broken furniture that I find in every garage sale at home.

It's no use to repeat the funny sounds we made bargaining in our respective languages, but a fair price was finally reached. After the deal was made, the seller served us cold, delicious Puerto Rican pineapple, an amenity you never get in local garages.

How to bargain at garage sales. It's only a little different, a little less serious, than bargaining in the antiques shops. I never haggle over an item that costs pennies. That way I feel like a big spender and I earn the good will of the seller in case I want something that runs high.

Start like this: accumulate a few things before you try to knock down the aggregate price. Be very genteel about it; the opening is your trump card: "Are your prices firm?" or "Can we negotiate price?" or "I have a few things here—can I get a better price?" In other words, ask, don't tell them what to charge for very cheap merchandise. On higher priced items, follow my bargaining instructions in chapter 4.

If the seller has something you dearly want but can't afford, make her a reasonable offer. Write it on a piece of paper with your name and telephone number and tell her you'll be back at the end of the sale. If she can't get a better price in the meantime, she may just sell the piece to you.

Keep a sense of humor. It helps to have it when the bargaining begins. If you're a friendly person you should do well at garage sales. If you're not friendly, the free and easy atmosphere may thaw you out. The homespun humor repeats over and over:

"Is everything for sale?"
"Everything but my husband."
    or

"Do you have any antiques?"
"Only my wife."

Another joke you keep hearing is the complaint gag about buying too much: "I bought and bought; I can't resist a bargain; now I need a garage sale of my own!"

The amateur huckster is funny without trying: "This pot can boil, broil, fry, poach, bake, roast, anything! It's been in my family for three generations, my grandmother lived to be a hundred in it—"

"How much is it?"

"Twenty-five cents; take it before I change my mind, I'm sentimental . . ."

The fun peters out before closing time. You happen to notice the "Garage Sale" sign so you stop and go in. You're the only buyer and you're wishing you weren't. The owner and a neighbor are sitting in glum silence scrutinizing you as carefully as if you're on the FBI's Most-Wanted List. You're almost obliged to buy something, anything, or slink out in a self-imposed state of original sin. Your only advantage in coming so late is that the proprietress might reduce some ridiculously high-priced item—*if* the sale isn't continuing the next day.

Types of merchandise. The range is incredible. I'll never give up on garage sales because I don't know what I'll find next. Antiques aren't the only lure: even the most confirmed antiquer gets hooked sooner or later on other garage sale products.

Here's a sampling of what I've purchased: real old gold, and/or silver eyeglass frames that have become popular for wearing or displaying, doilies, antiques of all classifications, advertising items, picture frames, paintings, a variety of glassware, plants, planters, cutlery, perfume, jewelry (old and new), furniture, lamps, beer steins, candlesticks, ceramic ware, chopsticks, scarves, small electrical appliances, dresses, silver, hardware, cosmetics, thick cotton electrical gloves, dolls. Anything you can buy in the stores, you can buy here.

Prices. Prices may start at ten cents but they can go as high as several hundred dollars when, for instance, quality furniture or antiques are being offered. A high price can still be a bargain if the merchandise is desirable and in good condition. You have to exercise caution before buying.

However, there's an abundance of items for a dollar and under. Not long ago I paid a dollar for an unused $8.50 combination can opener and knife sharpener. The owner moaned into my ear, "There's three more of them—presents—in the house. No one thinks I can cook!"

I bought a fifty-cent carnival glass fruit bowl that was selling for five dollars in the antiques shops. But my prize in glass was a tremendous, footed, partly-pressed, partly-cut glass bowl that cost me twenty-five cents because it had a tiny chip in its rim that pained the owner.

I used to feel guilty about buying absurdly low-priced antiques and collectibles. But in the course of time I've learned that some people attach no value to their old pieces, especially if they come out of a dusty attic. To them it's a miracle that you're paying for their junk. And don't worry, when they sell a high quality piece, they charge more.

Emotional stimulus. Garage selling is a positive profession. There's not enough money involved for seller or buyer to be unpleasant. Buyers come in twos and threes; it's almost like a picnic. For sellers, which I've also been, it's equally exhilarating, mostly because of the profit.

It's hard to describe the high you get. Just being there is exciting. But finding a treasure for practically no money is a thrill that lasts all day. You'll babble to everyone who wants to listen. There's a lot of babbling at garage sales.

Besides thrills, you can also get emotional fulfillment. It comes from person-to-person contact. I remember some of these people for a long time afterward. Because of the variety of personalities you come across, some leave a greater-than-usual impact. I'm reminded immediately of a young woman with a smile that welcomed the world. Among her sales items was a solid, slightly peeling, formerly all-gilt nineteenth-century Eastlake-style masonry something-or-other, decorated with three ferocious lions; presumably it was a candleholder. I loved it immediately.

"How much do you want for it?" I asked the seller, whose sunny face was the antithesis of those three hoary lions.

"Make me an offer."

"A dollar!"

"It's yours, and don't ask me what the thing is." We touched hands momentarily as the money was exchanged, and something good, if intangible, passed between two strangers. Yes, it could have been love, fed by possession and profit. I lingered a few minutes to ask about my new purchase and our conversation was altogether happy, perhaps because it was brief, uncomplicated, and final. Maybe finality is the secret of garage sale happiness.

Garage-sale furniture. Used furniture, I've been told by experts, depreciates by one-half its value the day after it's been used. This may be true, but are you going to turn down something that's been well kept, unscratched, is made of great wood, and whose craftsmanship is fine, because people are asking more than half the original price? And how do you get to know the original price? You don't. The secret of buying old furniture from private owners is to shop in the furniture stores, new and used, to get a rundown of market prices before you bargain.

You can furnish a whole house inexpensively by following the classified ads. In addition to garage and estate sales, the "House Furnishings" section covers just about everything in used furniture. I feel that the best buys in this market are the sturdy, attractive stock built forty to sixty years ago. It's too young to be expensive, but not young enough to be jerry-built.

There's also a healthy variety of antique furniture available, or rather the semi-antique turn-of-the-century type we can still afford. (Quality antiques run into thousands of dollars.) Take my open whatnot cabinet, a garage-sale item. It's mahogany, with a bevel-edged mirror on top and the original sticker recommending Sweet Home Soap on the back. It was lovely, and was being sold by a woman conducting her own garage sale from a big beautiful house in an elite neighborhood. (Garage sales are everywhere.)

"Don't bargain with me," was her doorway greeting, "I'd rather give it all to charity." I hadn't said a word.

I was attracted to the whatnot immediately.

"I bought it years ago from someone who told me it belonged to Teddy Roosevelt."

I had a friend along, also an antiques buff. She wasn't shy. "Then why don't you give it to the Smithsonian Institution?"

"Uh, how much—do you want?" I was cowed already by this reputed "T.R." possession.

"Twenty-five dollars; I won't take a cent less."

"We'll give you twenty dollars cash—now! it'll be out of here in ten minutes," my nervy friend answered.

Well, I got it for $21.50, and still can't believe it.

Antique furniture prices have a way of fluctuating according to the whims and personalities of the sellers. But you'll always get your money back. A good antique can only go up in value.

Estate sales. If you delight in the flavor of antiques combined with garage sales, history, intimate lifestyles, personalities and bargains, this is it. An estate sale gives you the run of the house. From basement to attic, you can explore to your heart's content, poking your hot little hands into each nook and cranny in the building. A person has died and the executors are settling the estate by selling every last one of the deceased's possessions. They will advertise the sale in the classified columns of local newspapers or perhaps in one metropolitan newspaper.

Like a department store, there's different merchandise on different floors. There are tools in the basement; antiques, furniture, books, and china at ground level; clothes and bedroom furniture upstairs; and everything else is in the attic. Nobody will stop you from hanging around as long as you spend money.

Professional garage salers. These are individuals (often dealers) who run your sale for a portion (usually 50 percent) of the profits. Prices are higher than those charged by amateurs, but lower than in antiques shops. The merchandise is generally of a good quality, with junk consigned to the bargain basement.

Only in the last two or three years have I become aware of the pros. They use trade names, call their ventures "tag" sales, and operate from the owner's home. As middlewomen (mostly), they fix prices, arrange publicity, advertise the sale in newspapers, tag every item, police the house, take cash, answer questions, do the bookkeeping, and so on. Their function is to remove the burden of the sale from the inexperienced, often well-to-do, greedy housewife. She used to call the Salvation Army when she was changing homes. Now she liquidates second-hands with the aid of a financial wizard.

As an example of the good buys you can get at these sales, I recently paid a dollar for a nicely decorated invalid feeder (a small pitcher-like dish with an extra long spout, like Pinocchio's nose). Most invalid feeders cost a lot more because they are so scarce. I also bought a miniature hand-enameled, hand-blown antique cranberry bottle for two dollars.

Mundane considerations.

(a) One of the most important of these is how to find your way to a sale. Most advertisers list their addresses without giving directions (in an ad, every word costs money). If you have to drive, and you almost always do, stop at a garage near your destination. Hanging on the office wall (smudged by greasy fingers) is a local map with a legend, where you'll quickly locate the place of sale. But move fast; if you don't, the mechanics will develop a strange compulsion to help you and will, of course, delay you.

(b) Don't doll up for the occasion. Dress down or you'll feel uncomfortable. This is penny ante stuff, not Las Vegas.

(c) Bring lots of loose change and small bills. Most proprietors start with a lot of change but they often run out.

(d) Don't be intimidated by the lack of other buyers if you arrive early or late. You're not obliged to buy something, anything, to help out. If you're early, you may want to buy. If you're late, you have learned your lesson but you're still not obliged to buy. Just smile sweetly, say "thank you," and walk away.

(e) Don't buy before prices are affixed to items. That's a sure way of getting overcharged.

(f) The dead of winter—January, February, March—is understandably off-season for outdoor sales in cold climates. Follow the sun to Florida. Or simmer down; there are still enough rummage sales, indoor sales, and auctions to keep you going.

There's always another. If you need a positive, soul-supporting philosophy, this is it. It means that disappointments are inevitable, but so are garage sales. Whenever I leave a place empty-handed and low-spirited, I say to myself, "There's always another." And there always is.

6
Just Plain Folks

I came across some of my nicest cheap antiques a few doors away from me. They'd been lying under my nose for years and I had never suspected it. This is the unbelievable story I promised you in Chapter 2. It opened up a new source of supply which I call "Just Plain Folks," or how to buy antiques directly from people rather than through the usual merchandising arenas. Not even the classifieds can help you here, because most of my "plain folks" haven't thought of selling, let alone advertising. However, after you've given them the idea, they're very happy to let go of their unwanted pieces at reasonable prices.

I was cleaning out my garage one summer day, aided by two young unwilling volunteers, my children. They were singing and laughing in spite of their bondage, and the noise radiated in every direction. We soon had a visitor from the house in back.

"What's going on?" It was Mildred, a middle-aged widow who had lived there alone since her husband died. Because she worked I didn't see much of her, but I admired her independence and strength of mind.

"We're making room for the car."

"We're making room for more antiques," corrected one of my geniuses.

"You know, I have stuff like this in my garage." Mildred poked distastefully at a small oak chair which I had stored here prior to refinishing it.

"Oh yes?" I noted politely, not yet tuned in to what she was communicating.

"And a big slab of marble that Jack was going to use for a table top before he died. And some other garbage he collected; he was always collecting—"

Suddenly my antennas rose. "Jack collected?"

"Oh sure. I never liked that stuff, except a few things we kept in the house."

"Well maybe—maybe . . . I'd like to see your garage. Maybe, that is . . ." I wanted to say that maybe I'd buy some of it, but I wasn't talking to a dealer and for a change I was tongue-tied. How did you wheel and deal with a neighbor?

"Come on over; you'll tell me what to throw away." She looked meaningfully at my oak chair.

"Oh no, that's a good chair, an antique."

"You're kidding."

"I'll be glad to look at your things!" I was very excited by now. The possibilities had finally hit home. I wasn't even insulted by her open dislike of my treasures. It was the old story, "one man's meat is another man's poison."

We walked back to her garage, opened the door, and there I was face to face with a gorgeous clutter of tables, chairs, headboards, odd furniture, and odd boxes and bags. At first I moved slowly, but soon I became careless from anticipation and tripped over a small paper bag half full of something.

You won't believe this even after I say it. The something in that bag on the floor turned out to be the dome half of a heavy old cut and pressed crystal cheese dish, the kind with a faceted round ball on top. If I'd only known about Jack's collecting habit I'd have found that dome before it got chipped on the inside edge, probably as a result of being kicked around the garage floor.

"It's—beautiful." I was breathless.

"Say, I think I have the bottom plate for that in the house."

"What else do you have in those paper bags?"

"I hated this glass thing; threw it in here after a while—"

"I'll buy it from you."

"No!"

"You won't sell it?"

"You mean you'll pay good money for that?!"

I gave her an education in antiques, after which we opened every—and I do mean every—paper bag on the garage floor. I sorted out the antiques from the new stuff and then I called in a dealer who lived nearby. Mildred knew her by sight. I couldn't price the items objectively because I wanted so many of them. The dealer and Mildred set prices, with me hovering protectively in the background. I had first choice, but the dealer took the lion's share because she could sell them.

It was a perfect arrangement. I was ecstatic over my cheese dish and other items, Mildred was ecstatic over the money we gave her, and the dealer presumably made hers back with a profit.

You too can find treasures in your neighbor's home. You may not stumble over a bag of crystal as an introduction to merchandising; you may have to inquire around; and if you're easily embarrassed you may have to give it up. On the other hand, you may find a willing seller right next door. You don't have to be ashamed. You're not asking for money; you're offering it. Try the older people first; they have older pieces. And especially try the retirees before someone else gets to them.

I previously suggested that you knock on strange doors along country roads if you want to find a dusty heirloom that nobody's thought about for years. You can't do this sort of thing in the city or suburbs for several reasons:

1. People are afraid to open their doors; they may even call the police.
2. Urban people are wise to antiques; they'd soak you.
3. Right after your first words (through metal or wood), you'd be pegged as a crackpot and treated accordingly.

I almost bought a couple of pressed glass pieces from an old lady in a not quite rural farmhouse. An "almost" story doesn't count, but I'm telling it because I want you to know that I've already knocked on strange doors. I'm not one of those wiseguys who tells you what to do but won't do it myself.

The farm was what you'd call "a vanishing American phenomenon," the kind you sometimes find near much-trafficked suburban roadways. I went there in the summer to buy home-grown tomatoes and red peppers. The idea of soliciting antiques didn't occur to me until I saw an older woman in an apron come out of the house one afternoon. She might have old glass! flashed the inspirational message as I followed her back into the house with my eyes.

I didn't have the nerve to knock that day; the idea was too fresh. But I knew I'd have to try soon. So I served tomatoes for breakfast, lunch, and dinner until the supply ran out. And then I went back for more.

I was afraid the old lady, whoever she was, wouldn't be there. I'd seen young fellows around and I didn't want to deal with them. The last time I'd rung a farm bell was out in the real countryside. A bunch of men, most of them young, were cleaning implements at the side of the barn, and they beckoned me over. When I told them I wanted antiques, the reactions were great fun—for them. They said that everything in the house was old, but they couldn't sell me the floors and walls. And other things like that. I got away as fast as I could.

This time I rang the bell hesitantly and was glad to see the same old lady come to the door. When I asked about old glass (I had decided to be specific), she studied me for a moment and said, yes, she had a few old things, and ushered me through the pantry into the kitchen. It was an old undecorated room. She opened what was probably the original cupboard and pulled out a few pieces of glass.

"This what you mean?"

They were surely old pressed glass pieces. One of them had a flashed ruby rim, the sort of thing being reproduced today. All were undistinguished and unpretty, and I could see why she didn't display them.

"Well—I—how much money are you asking for them?" I couldn't say no thank you right away, not after taking the woman out of her routine with my unorthodox request.

"Now, I haven't thought about that; never thought about selling them. I don't know if I want to sell them."

What a relief! I was about to slink away with apologies when a man walked in.

"Here's my brother; he owns the farm. This lady wants to buy my glass that mama left," she misrepresented.

He looked at me like I was crazy. "Well, I don't know. Don't ask me. You want to sell it?"

"I don't know. What's it worth?"

"I don't know."

"We'd have to see what it's worth, and maybe I'd sell it, maybe I wouldn't," she mused, "but say—do you have an idea what it's worth?"

"I think, maybe . . ." I was struggling to come up with an honest evaluation when I realized I didn't have to. "Well, I don't know enough about this kind of glass, but I'd be interested to know," I lied. "You find out and I'll come back."

I was out of there like a bullet. We didn't eat those particular tomatoes and red peppers for the rest of the summer, and I felt guilty for months afterward.

I've knocked on various doors during trips and summer vacations and I've picked up a few pieces of old glass and china. I'm sure I could do much better if I traveled a lot and if my family were willing to tolerate this madness. I know other people who've been very successful at ringing rural bells, especially people who collect antiques professionally. It's a matter of experience, application, and aggressiveness.

In dealing with sellers, the less talking you do, the better. You don't have to volunteer your knowledge about antiques. Let the owners do all the necessary research they need to help them determine prices. Learn to be a good listener. That way you won't wind up looking out for the other guy's interests rather than your own. This false do-goodism has managed to kill a few very promising deals for me. In one such case I was the first to arrive at a child's garage sale. As usual, I was totally disinterested in recent toys and other children's knickknacks. But the mother and I started a lively conversation about garage sales in general, and we were enjoying ourselves.

While we talked, a few youngsters came up with their contributions to what was actually a cooperative venture among friends. They began jockeying for best position, everybody feverish with the prospect of making money. We almost missed the arrival of a next-door neighbor who had been invited to participate. Since she hadn't played with toys for at least fifty years, her merchandise was more interesting to me.

"I love that little end table," said the mother of the major entrepreneur; "how much do you want for it, Jennie?"

"Well, I don't know. It's old and very sturdy. But it needs a refinishing. I don't know what to ask; what do you think?" Her look swept across the two of us but I wasn't one to interfere with financial negotiations.

They came to some sort of agreement while I examined the rest of Jennie's furniture.

"You have some nice pieces," I verified, "but I don't need furniture. Do you have anything else to sell?"

They exploded into laughter so spontaneous that I had to know what was behind it. And this was the story: Jennie had inherited boxes and parcels of bric-a-brac from her dead aunt, and it had laid dormant in her garage for years (another garage treasure, but well packed). Meantime she and her disabled mother, both widowed, lived alone together in the house, which was filled with a combined accumulation of their own bric-a-brac and furnishings. They were now selling the house and looking for an apartment. So when I asked if she had anything else to sell, it was like asking Niagara if it had water.

"I started to unpack the cartons this morning. But I can't get rid of anything until I ask my daughters what they want. Come on into the house; I'll show you some of my aunt's things—and I'll show you mine."

I, a virtual stranger, was then taken on a guided tour of Shangri-La. I saw old, brilliant, cut and marked crystal; oriental antiques, including a porcelain tea set; jade; elaborate cloisonné vases; miniature sterling salt dips (stored in a mayonnaise jar that was almost as old as the dips); a sheathed ancient Japanese sword; commemorative plates and glassware; every kind of pottery imaginable; a banjo; grandfather and Sevres clocks; Persian carpets; and other treasures. The rest of the house was casual, even neglected. The moving process had started, but Jennie didn't know exactly what to do with her things: "I don't even know what to sell them for."

"Nothing looks cheap," I volunteered. "For instance, the cloisonné vases: I'll bet they're worth hundreds of dollars."

"No!!"

"Well, sure; go to your library, look in the books. Now, for instance . . . ," and I ran down a few more prices on things I knew pretty well, punctuated by her occasional, "I don't believe it!" or "That much?" By the time I finished I had Jennie in a very reflective mood.

"If you decide to sell . . . there are a couple of pieces I'd love; but only if you decide . . ." What a puny speech! That was the moment I should have forged ahead, offered money, and secured a few prizes for myself. A forceful person could have made a deal; I killed it. Instead I gave her my phone number and she promised she'd call me first, out of gratitude.

Well, I didn't hear from Jennie for weeks. I became anxious. What if she'd lost my phone number? I hated to bother her but I couldn't get her antiques out of my mind. I was saving my money like crazy. I called her.

"Oh no, I didn't lose it—it's right here next to the phone." Then she told me about the apartment she'd rented, how the packing was going and so on. I was preening myself on our rapport when she dropped the bomb, "Yes, I'll certainly have a sale, but it won't be my antiques." Not her antiques! What had I done?

I'll tell you what I did. I did such a thorough job of convincing her she had valuable antiques that she decided to keep the pieces her daughters didn't want, and wait for prices to go up, up, up. I had only myself to blame.

Jennie was another example of the "Just Plain Folks" you can discover by using your own initiative. I spoiled that transaction myself, through my ignorance of proper business conduct. At other times when you work person-to-person you can be taken advantage of and deliberately used by the other party, through lies and various devices over which you have no control.

I met one of these schemers while we were walking through a local estate sale. She approached me and another woman in a very friendly fashion, commenting on the confusing range of prices, asking, "How do you know what to charge?" The other woman wasn't to be distracted from her buying frenzy but I sensed something more in the first woman's question than met the ears. And I was right. She soon revealed that she would be selling her late father-in-law's effects at her own sale in a few weeks.

JUST PLAIN FOLKS

Don't ask me how I got to her garage a few blocks away. I woke up and suddenly I was there. (Maybe I was hypnotized.) And because I couldn't resist acting like an expert, this oh-so-innocent lady picked and picked my brains about her father-in-law's possessions until I realized I was doing it again. I stopped talking, too late.

"You've been very kind," she said; "I'd like you to have first choice on the antiques. Give me your phone number." Where had I heard that offer before! Well, guess what, she called me last, after the antiques dealers had combed the place. They left her with a few undesirable pieces for which she needed a sucker—me. But I didn't know all this until I got there and asked questions. The only satisfaction I derived, aside from not buying anything, was that she must have given the stuff away. Dealers pay as little as they can.

Now when I deal with people, known or unknown, it's strictly business. I take the soothing approach that they don't owe me anything, not even a phone call. By the same token, I don't owe them an evaluation. I've decided to credit them with being able to price their own belongings, without my help. We remain cordial from beginning to end. In that way we can transact business and I can still regard "Just Plain Folks" as a good source of supply.

The moral of all this is, you have to push and pry and poke into places where you don't belong; but you have to do it with a light touch, a friendly face, and a strong sense of determination. Once you start doing business, the tone should become formal and mercantile, no matter how friendly you've been before. Let the seller do the selling while you listen. You may want to bargain afterward, but not until *she* sets the price. If she insists on help with the pricing, and you desperately want the piece, quote an absurdly low amount; you'll see how fast she counters with the price she's had in the back of her mind all along. Some of these transactions won't come off; most of them will.

7
Auctions

The funniest thing I ever saw at an auction, where humor is intertwined with the hard sell, like lovers, was a bid made from a passing car. It was a blowy summer's day in suburbia. The audience faced the auctioneer across the twisting corner lawn of the house whose furnishings were being auctioned. Some of our low-keyed bids had been carried off by the wind, so we were forced to yell or wave our arms.

The auctioneer was holding up a tall signed art glass vase decorated with showy iridescent peacock feathers whose outrageous colors glared back at us through the afternoon sun.

"Twenty-five!" Dollars, the auctioneer had already given us to understand. He had also let us know it was a ridiculously low starting sum, and he had no intention of allowing it to languish there.

He got his price from a dozen hands. Encouraged by this vigorous enthusiasm for the beautiful vase, he decided to bypass his previous two-and-a-half-dollar progression and shouted the next number as "Thirty!"

The same hands went up.

"I have thirty in a dozen places. Oh, this is nice, very nice; let's hurry and make it thirty-five; do I hear thirty-five?" and he laughed delightedly, anticipating a real run-up, smelling money as if it were baking in the oven.

The vase shot up in price, passing the hundred-five-dollar mark, with the bidding field only slightly narrowed.

The auctioneer was feeling no pain. "One hundred and ten dollars from number fifty-one; do I hear one hundred fifteen? I do?" He looked at another hot bidder and got the go-ahead. "Yes, yes; and now we're at one hundred twenty—from—from number fifty-one again, which brings us to the magic money mark of one hundred twenty-five dollars. Do I hear one hundred twenty-five lovely green bills?" he shouted in competition with a sudden gust of wind.

"One hundred fifty!!" roared an audacious male bidder from no identifiable location. This was not an unheard-of ploy at auctions. Still and all, we wanted to see the unknown capitalist who had so wantonly overturned the guidelines. Necks began to stretch almost at the same time as the tittering began.

"It was that car!" a woman pointed. I followed her index finger in time to catch a bright red convertible driving leisurely down the block with four young laughing faces looking back at us and mocking us and our numbers game.

The sputtering auctioneer could only echo, "From th-that car?" as he was informed about the joke. He seemed disoriented, his hopes for a hot new competition dashed. He lamely brought the bidding to a close at $145, which was probably much less than he had anticipated. The joy of money-making had deserted the corpulent auctioneer after the audacious hoax had been played.

This is by way of illustrating that auctions are held everywhere. In cold weather they're usually indoors, but in summer they can be indoors or out. Summer auctions are held in barns or auction halls, night or

AUCTIONS

day; or they may be next to a cow pasture during the day. You'll sometimes find animals being sold alongside the antiques. You usually have to bring your own chair for the cheap auctions, but you can buy lunch if you're too lazy to prepare it.

The auction's location often determines its general price range. I mentioned in Chapter 2 that some country auctions are held under tents in upper-middle-class areas. Bids in the hundreds of dollars are the rule here. I consider this a middle-range sale, with a few items going for less than $100 and a few bringing in thousands. The middle-range auction is a standard feature of many permanent city auction houses as well. City auction houses will probably guarantee the age and authenticity of their products. Some other reliable city auctioneers in the middle price range travel from motel to hotel for their sales; others work out of private homes and warehouses.

All these auctions rely heavily on advertising to pull in the crowds. But don't let them get you: bear in mind that the middle-range auction isn't for you except as a form of entertainment and for a rare purchase. It's too expensive. The same holds true for the high-priced sale. In this latter category are, for instance, the house auctions of a Rockefeller or Morgan. These are the ones that get written up in the newspapers before and after the sale. Lists of breathtaking items are published. Just to get in can cost you as much as the fifteen-dollar catalogue fee. The catalogue price substitutes as an admission fee. If this fee is high enough it will guarantee bona fide buyers and exclude penniless rubber-neckers like you and me. Somebody may be lucky enough to get a doorknob for twenty-five dollars, but most of the fine objets d'art are sold at prices ranging from the upper hundreds to the upper thousands.

High prices also prevail at the best auction houses in the world's largest cities, such as at Parke-Bernet and Sotheby's. I won't say more about such places because you have to be rich to bid. You even have to get someone else to bid for you; it's a cabalistic ritual that one can't hope to learn without the proper initiation rites.

So let's get back to cheap auctions. These are for you. You'll find them in city, suburban, and rural auction halls; in motels and hotels; churches and synagogues; civic and social club halls; in warehouses, and in barns; and in private homes. I've attended auctions in all of these places.

Sometimes there's an admission fee, and sometimes there's not. If there's a charitable sponsoring organization you may have to pay a dollar or more to get in, which may or may not include the catalogue. But the auction is worth the money because of its entertainment value. The auctioneers are a show in themselves, and the bidders are often unintentionally funny.

The cheapest auctions are rarely catalogued. Most of them are held by groups sponsoring special causes, such as as-yet incurable illnesses. The membership of the organization donates or procures sales items, and they have one or two favorite auctioneers who know how to make the most of their junk.

A rule of thumb to guide you at cheap auctions is that prices should range from twenty-five cents to about fifty dollars. However, I've seen antiques sold for well over their market value at cheap auctions, especially those held by religious institutions. I think this is because there's a large congregational attendance and there are few dealers. Members tend to be overly zealous in bringing in the money while dealers try to hold prices down.

Sitting gracefully under a tree in my backyard is a horse and buggy seat (minus the buggy) which I bought dearly at a cheap auction in a church. The seat is made of sturdy green wood with an undulating black wrought iron support at the bottom. I should love it for its evocation of days gone by and the fact that its

AUCTIONS

likeness will never be reproduced in today's market. But every time the tenderness wells up in my heart it gets pushed down by remembrance of how I lost control during the bidding.

This was one church auction where prices were really cheap. It may have been that the worshipers were boycotting this crass subservience to mammon. A lovely old bird's-eye maple chest of drawers with original hardware went for eight dollars, innumerable pieces of antique glass and china stayed under the five-dollar level, and so on.

I wanted only the buggy seat, nothing else. When they finally brought it out I thought my heart would blow a gasket from joy.

"We'll start this fine old wagon seat—a genuine antique—at five dollars. Any bidders, any bidders?"

Hands went up all around the auditorium.

Oh-oh, my heart pounded, oh-oh, oh-oh, in a steady grinding palpitation. Things didn't look good. Too many people wanted it.

I laid low while the first bids rolled on.

"Do I hear twelve and a half dollars, twelve and a half?" The competition was dwindling.

At fifteen dollars, more bidders went out. I came in at $17.50. By the time the bidding had reached $22.50, there were only four of us left.

During a hot run like this I'll usually examine my opponents' faces to gauge their determination. If it's tremendous, I'll stop bidding. This time I didn't look. I wanted the seat too much.

"Thirty dollars, thirty dollars!" offered the auctioneer, and then there were three of us. My mind was swimming in the dark waters of Lethe, the Greek river of oblivion. Forgotten were the vows of poverty and economy I took in my pursuit of antiques, as well as the perpetually low state of my finances. I was drowning.

"Thirty-two fifty, thirty-two fifty!!" Three hands.

"Thirty-five dollars!" Two hands.

"Thirty-seven fifty!!" My hand shot out automatically. My muscles were tight; my face felt taut and set.

"Going, going—" the inevitable rap of the amateur's mallet, "gone!" No opposition? Somewhere inside my head was the sure knowledge that I'd won the prize. But why, why didn't I feel exhilarated? Because I realized in the wake of my monomania that I'd been taken—and with less than forty dollars to my name, all of it earmarked for food.

"What are you going to do with it?" inquired my final adversary as I was paying.

"Oh, paint it white probably, and sit it in my backyard." But my spirit was dead, along with my love for wagon seats.

"Exactly what I had in mind. Until I took a good look at your face. You were so . . . determined. That's why I dropped out."

A smart woman. She did exactly what I should have done—sooner.

I never painted the seat white. I'd lost the feeling. But my husband was very excited about it. "Leave it green!" he insisted. He thought it was cheap, as wagon seats go. We worked out the money problem together, which would have thrilled me at any other time. But I still felt cheated. I'd succumbed to auction fever. It's as bad as the flu. And I wasn't even a congregationist.

Because it's so devastatingly easy to work yourself up at auctions, you should learn how to bid. Don't bid at your first auction. Just study the buyers. After a while you'll know the various types, including the overbidders, the dealers, the amateur collectors, the professional collectors, the dilettantes.

When you get to the actual bidding, make it a permanent rule to go slowly. Keep your mouth shut as soon as the auctioneer gives the opening price. He'll lower it if he gets no response. Wait for the strategic moment to start bidding, which you'll sense after you've attended enough auctions. Try not to sound enthusiastic, because it works up competitive interest in an item. And don't panic-bid when others are going after something you want. There are shills (employees of the auctioneer who specialize in bidding the boob beyond his means) in the audience waiting like alligators to swallow you and your money whole.

You'll do best at auctions if you study prices beforehand. Take your price guide to the inspection of merchandise, which is open to the public for an hour or so before the sale. Set an absolute sum as your ceiling bid and stick to it.

Another good auction technique is to follow the dealers' bidding. But be careful: a few of them here and there bid high because they run more expensive establishments. I learned that at one of my early auctions.

It took place in a warehouse. The merchandise had been removed from a bankrupt antique shop. Most of the people in the audience were dealers, lured by a wide selection of antiques. They were chatting amiably (I was listening around) until the bidding started, and then you should have seen the fur fly! Those who owned low-priced stores were keeping the bids down. It was great for me. I bought a cobalt-blue antique porcelain chocolate pot for eight dollars and two gloriously old brass Chinese incense burners for four; all were worth much more.

But it was when the gorgeous better pieces appeared that professional jealousy poisoned the atmosphere. A web of acquisition was being spun by a bejeweled black widow spider lady with lots of cash. By the time she had grabbed up the Tiffany pieces, the Art Deco jewelry, and the bronze animals, people were buzzing, "Who is she?" Those in the know said she owned a fancy shop on New York City's upper east side.

"I can't get my hands on any of that stuff—she outbids me—nothing . . ." whined a heavy woman in an old gray coat and kerchief.

I sat by with no money and objectively watched the slaughter. The spider lady won a lot of prizes. There are no laws limiting how much a person may buy at an auction. If she has a thick skin and if she owns a shop whose prices are high, she can afford to buy whatever she fancies. It's just as well that you don't know in advance that such a person will appear at a sale. You might stay away and miss out on some of the pieces she scorns, such as my chocolate pot. Nobody, but nobody, buys up a whole antiques auction—at least I haven't seen it happen at any sales I've attended.

The locale of the auction is sometimes a clue as to the type of product it offers. As a general rule, the warehouse or moving and storage auction features the kind of household goods people put into storage and forget: lots of furniture and sealed cartons of smaller items, like dishes. Furniture is probably the best bargain. It can't be carried off as easily as small pieces; hence it brings relatively lower prices.

An auction that's held on the premises of a closed-up antiques shop features antiques exclusively. But a general auction held in a motel, hotel, or auction hall draws its merchandise from many sources, including private homes and estates, antiques shops, other auctions, and wholesalers, and offers a much wider range of goods. The ads may say "antiques," and antiques may be included, but they're only part of it.

Benefit auctions which are staged in various types of institutional buildings have the widest variety of products, whose condition range from brand new to terrible. Because of the wide scope of these sales, I like to know that the auctioneer is trustworthy. (You'll get to sense which of them are honest and which are not after you've gone to enough auctions in a given area.) An honest auctioneer will tell you what's wrong with the items; he'll indicate which ones are antiques and which are reproductions; he'll start the bidding at the right price; he'll refund your money if the piece has been misrepresented; he usually won't accept sealed bids, a practice that allows non-attenders to win auction pieces by submitting bids long before the actual bidding starts.

My favorite auction locale is the private home. I love the personal touch. The idea that things have stood in a certain place for a long time makes me think of them as being genuine. If the pieces look old enough, they were probably passed down through a few generations.

The best house auction I ever went to involved the estate of a red-hot collector. The house had been owned by a middle-aged divorcée whose greatest joy was to buy. She filled four floors with more inanimate objects than I'd ever believed it was possible to see outside a department store.

"She was a compulsive buyer," her brother explained. She lived alone in the large home and needed every room to store her purchases. They poured out of drawers, onto and under beds, up the walls, and on the walls; some things even hung from the ceilings. Windows were embellished with high-quality curtains and drapes that were pulled aside to display windowsills teeming with tiny knickknacks. You couldn't see the furniture tops for the bric-a-brac. There were dolls and other figurines, china and porcelain pieces, radios of every variety, cosmetic jars, perfume bottles and glass pieces too numerous to mention, pictures in frames, trays, lamps, books and bookends, banks, doilies, paintings and other art work. It would be folly to try to describe all she had. If I tell you some of the more bizarre things you'll get the idea:

1) At least sixty wristwatches for every occasion, as well as a dozen or so exquisite antique pocket and lapel watches
2) Seventeen separate and complete sets of dishes, including a full set of Japanese dinnerware, vintage 1930

3) Four antique china closets crammed with cut and pressed glass only
4) Seven jewelry boxes crammed with good costume pieces
5) Two closets crammed with shoes alone
6) Twenty-five separate large tapestries piled up on a table.

She wasn't a rich woman, but she had a good job and no responsibilities. She had lived in the house all her life, inheriting it and some of its contents from her parents. Money was no problem so she developed an expensive avocation, the art of buying.

It took three days to auction the contents of that property, and another two days for us to collect our purchases. What a complex bookkeeping system the procedure required! My major acquisition was a four-fold hand-painted Japanese screen with a black lacquered frame, the kind that costs a hundred dollars today. I paid $17.50 for it. The original sixty-dollar price tag was still on the back. I also bought a magnificent wooden bow (five dollars—no arrows) for my son, which gives you an idea of the diversity of this lady's possessions.

The majority of house auctions are in a price range you can afford, anywhere from a dollar and up. Bidding on antiques can get hot, but since many of the people who attend are like you, and many are dealers, prices rarely get really exorbitant. Also, you can trust most of the merchandise that's reputed to be old or antique. So have fun, and good luck!

8
Flea Markets

I was at a large flea market early one summer day while the morning breezes were still blowing. Exhibitors were unpacking, but so far I hadn't seen anything that gripped me by the throat. I'd been wandering around for a while along with other onlookers—they get crowded early—when I decided to try a different tactic. So I stopped short and scanned the length and breadth of the grounds for the most promising cluster of buyers.

There were several. I suddenly found myself saying "eenie-meenie" like a kid in a candy store. Flea markets do that to me; they bring out a youthful exuberance that goes hand in hand with the excitement of looking for antiques. "My mother told me to pick this one." I was sure my hocus-pocus would pay off with fabulous treasures, so I rushed to the chosen spot.

By the time I reached it, a dozen or more people were circling around whatever was in the middle. Trying to get one small peek was like bucking a solid wall. "There must be diamonds here," I thought. I'm not an aggressive type, but I'm thin and I can coil in and out of people like a snake, unnoticed. This time it didn't work. One woman hissed, "Don't shove!" Another mumbled something about "getting there a minute later."

I dropped back to the edge of the crowd and cringed there quietly until attrition removed two people in front of me. After waiting a while, my common sense told me that nobody would leave while valuables were being unwrapped. Would I? I had to try getting to the center again, but now I would do it unobtrusively, passing one person at a time. I began my new strategy in a very ladylike way, but it needed a world of patience, which I didn't have at that moment, because time was flitting by.

I might have given up if the widely-built man blocking my view hadn't decided to leave (almost crushing me to death). Two of us filled his void. A moment later the crowd shifted and my vista became infinite.

You won't believe this.

That tenacious, gluttony-motivated group (myself included) was waiting for the privilege of seeing a spaniel bitch nursing three darling pups which were in the process of being sold. If you think I left immediately in disgust, you're wrong. I stood and watched the tender tableau as long as anyone else.

But don't let that heart-warming story discourage you from joining other such clusters throughout the United States. Flea markets are crawling and multiplying over our great country like cockroaches. Any excuse makes a flea market: ten neighbors banding together with the idea of making huge profits from the bargain-hunting public; the Campfire Girls looking for yet another source of income; local churches setting up selling booths and rides in their back parking lot; the various incorporated groups trying to combat diseases, selling merchandise to subsidize their activities; a bunch of semipro dealers with a fair to middling antiques inventory huddling together under an occasional roof; and lots of positive advertising to go along with these outfits.

FLEA MARKETS

Great bargains exist in all these markets; you have to learn how to find them. You have to pick and choose sales, mercilessly eliminating those that are undesirable. Either that or you'll do nothing for the rest of your life but run to flea markets.

There aren't any easy ways to figure out, sight unseen, which ones are good or bad. So how do you learn to choose? One way is experience. You go to a lot of wrong ones before you learn not to go back to them in the following years. And how do you know they're wrong? They are if you don't see a single bargain; if there's a jumble of garbage-y old pieces; if the merchandise is uniformly new and/or trashy, and there's not an antique in sight; or if the merchandise isn't quite new/isn't quite old/isn't quite anything—those flea markets aren't for the antiques collector.

When the same group sponsors next year's market, you more or less know not to go, unless you have an hour to waste and an irresolute mind. And if by some chance you pick up an old cut crystal sugar bowl for a dollar (I did at one such flea market), please don't send me a gloating letter. Chances are you'll go back for the next five years and find nothing.

I know your next question. Suppose the flea market is sponsored by a group you never heard of; should you go? Yes. Very definitely. There has to be a first time. After a while you'll get to know the sponsors. Some of them consistently produce second-rate merchandise and second-rate dealers. Others get an "A" rating almost every time. Again, it's a matter of nosing around until you gain enough experience to pick and choose.

A factor that will help you make up your mind is whether you have to pay admission. The combined "flea-antique" markets operating for a holy cause all charge through the nose, and their merchandise is costly. Other places that charge admission boast hundreds of dealers (pros and semipros), cover a tremendous spectrum of goods and prices, and have a lower entrance fee. These markets can be fun and informative for antiques seekers, and they may include a few cheap out-of-town sellers who have unusual and interesting goods. Finally, there's the annual church sale of nice, clean used goods of all descriptions, and which has a cheap admission because the sponsors know it's worthwhile. Go to this one.

Suburbanites and city dwellers each have their own typical flea markets. In both cases they're held week after week in the same place (unless weather forbids) and are given a descriptive overall name, such as the Big Apple Flea Market. These are advertised regularly in the newspapers. The city market is city-sized and overpriced. The suburban market is smaller and cheaper, and attracts amateur sellers. It also charges considerably less for selling space. Both types feature antiques alongside exhibits of contemporary merchandise.

Another kind of flea market you can take advantage of, and which I run to every time I'm away from home, is the small-town or big-highway-between-towns all-year-round market. These are usually tremendous in size and have a widespread reputation as well. They're open on weekends and holidays. All kinds of people sell here, though most are semipros. If you're a city or suburban dweller, you'll find prices a bit cheaper than the ones you're used to. The antique merchandise is also a bit different, depending on the area and its history. The sellers aren't city slickers but they're at least as much into antiques as you are. And it's an interesting experience to talk and listen to the sellers.

For instance, I was once captivated by a bottle man in New England. You couldn't count the number of bottles of every description he featured. And even though I'm not as interested in bottles as I am in fancy and/or functional antiques, I couldn't help gawking at his tremendous display—the range of marvelous old colors, the shapes, and above all, the antiquity of most of them.

"Aren't they something!" The woman next to me shared my sentiment. "They're so old! And they look so much better when they're dusty, don't they? Makes them more authentic."

"Well, they're dusty now cause they been sittin' around a bit," explained the seller, "but you should've seen some of these comin' out of the ground. Were they ever filthy!"

"Out of the ground?" I marveled. Here was a brand new source of antiques.

"That's where most old bottles come from, lady, excepting those that stayed in a family cause they fancied drinking their bitters out of certain bottles—"

"Bitters?"

"Well now, lady—" He licked his lips, as if preparing for a long talk, "Early Americans called their hard liquor 'bitters' so they could get out of payin' the whiskey taxes. And let me tell you, judging by the quantity of bitters bottles that's been dug up in these parts, there was plenty of unpaid taxes. You know where I found most of my bitters? Right under people's property. No sir, they didn't throw their bottles in the town dump; didn't want their neighbors to know how much they was drinking . . . that means I've had to work out of old property sites. It ain't easy readin' through local records, early books and maps, all kinds of papers. But that's how I know where to dig. Say lady, did you know that seventeenth-century homeowners built their barns first because their horses and cows were more important than the people? And that the people lived above the animals till they could build a house?"

When his speech was over I thanked him very enthusiastically (even though he hadn't quite convinced me to change my feelings about buying bottles), and walked away a little bit wiser about another aspect of antique collecting.

As a steady flea market patron, you'll need expertise in two areas: the feel of cheap antiques (or any antique), and a good memory for dealers' faces and dishonest practices. These take time to learn.

I'm not a card-carrying, diploma-bearing antiques expert, but I've gotten the feel of antiques from having bought so many. And since I can only afford the cheap kind, I've also gotten to know bargains when I see them. (I get my contact with high-quality old and ancient antiques from museums, books, shows, and a few antiques shops.) It's this "feel" you'll have to take with you when you visit the flea markets. Otherwise you'll wind up buying new items, thinking they're old. It's an easy mistake in a place where new and old are sold at adjoining tables, or even the same table.

These are some of the oldies I've acquired at flea markets recently, with their prices:

1) A pair of real coral and base metal early-twentieth-century earrings, one dollar
2) An old cut crystal sugar bowl, a dollar
3) A pair of cut steel shoe buckles (from 1920s), twenty-five cents
4) A man's base metal pocket watch chain, ten cents
5) A cane pattern cut glass early-twentieth-century perfume decanter with a cut-crystal round ball stopper, two dollars
6) Art Deco jewelry, including plastic clips for a quarter, bead necklaces ranging from twenty-five cents to a dollar, and a plastic hatpin (or scarf pin) with a screw-on safety piece at the pointed end for fifty cents.

Under no circumstances could any of the above have qualified as new items, and I felt confident about buying them. I didn't know most of the dealers I bought them from so I had to rely on my own knowledge and experience. If you get to know a dealer and trust her, that's even better. It's not hard to memorize faces after you've seen them enough. It may be a little more difficult for you to recognize their petty larcenies, but even these can be smoked out.

I personally think it's easier to know dealers and their quirks than it is to know merchandise. My first lesson on phoney dealers has stayed with me, because I see the man in question at most of the local flea markets to this day. I was a novice when I approached his table. He was unpacking, and in my innocence I thought him an absolute bumbler. Things were tumbling out of their wrappings in disarray as he muttered, "My wife knows where these belong; where did she go?" He dressed and acted like Charlie Chaplin's little bum. And that's what it was—an act. (But I didn't know it then.)

"How much is the necklace?" He had unique jewelry. I wanted the piece, but there was no price on it.

"You'll have to wait for my wife." He looked helpless, almost pathetic.

"I can't stay, I'm expecting company—"

"But I don't know." Would he cry?

"It's not gold or silver," I said, ingeniously.

"It's Art Deco; designer's name's on the catch."

"But I—"

"Sixteen dollars, not a cent less." Suddenly he was the self-sufficient hard bargainer. He didn't miss his wife at all. But what about the disorder and the Little Tramp routine? It wasn't until I saw him in clean clothes with a well-organized display at a very high-priced market that I rounded out the picture. The man was a master in the performing arts!

I'm sure this charlatan would have cheerfully cheated me, given a chance. I resist his diversified stock whenever I see him. I've learned who the honest dealers are and I go to them instead. It won't take long for you too to become comfortable at flea markets. And if local antiques in other parts of the country are unfamiliar at first sight, you'll soon get the feel of them from your broader antiques experiences. You'll also get to know dealer types, both honest and dishonest.

As a bonus, remember that flea markets sell brand-new merchandise at unbelievably low prices. You may never want to patronize your nearby retail shop again.

Illustrations

Most of the objects pictured in this section were bought within the year prior to publication. I chose these items because their prices are current and cheap.

The price of antiques is a funny thing. You can spend a lot of money or spend relatively little and not get a bargain. Or you can spend $25.00 on a jade lamp and $1.00 on an old golden oak chair and have two extraordinary bargains in spite of the $24.00 price difference. You have to know how to buy, which is what this book is all about.

Every photographed piece here is worth about five to ten times as much as I paid, give or take a dollar. If I'd bought these things for a higher price in the antique shops I wouldn't have been able to include them in this section. And if I'd continued to buy in the shops, as I did at first, I wouldn't have written this book.

Some of the items depicted are not antiques, in the strictest sense; they are not a hundred years old or more. They're a few years younger and known in the trade as collectibles, or semi-antiques, or just "old." They form the bulk of the merchandise in the average antique shop so I feel justified in using them to illustrate a book on antiques.

Photos courtesy of Pat J. Kozinski.

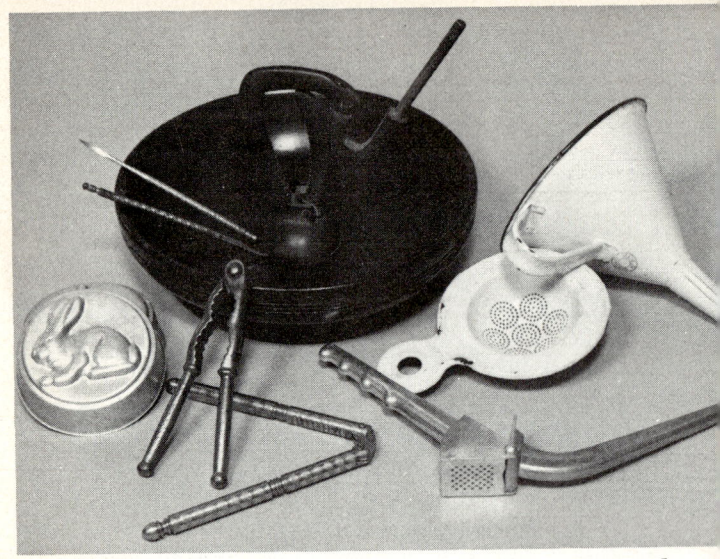

Five- Ten- and Twenty-five-Cent Kitchen Utensils
Identifiable with careful scrutiny are: an aluminum rabbit-outlined mold (left), two steel nutcrackers (bottom left) and nutpicks (in bowl), a mahogany bowl with built-in nutcracker (top), an aluminum lemon squeezer (bottom right), and a white granite strainer and funnel marked "Germany."

Facing page:

Furniture for All Seasons Furniture is another staple at all kinds of sales. As an explorer of dark corners at garage sales, I found this golden oak chair with carved back and solid seat in perfect condition, though covered with cobwebs. The owner said she hadn't planned to sell it, but I could have it for a dollar since she had no use for it.

Chinese Pure Silk Kimono   Second-hand clothes are what the rummage sale is all about.

I bought this silk kimono, or dressing gown, for $2.99 at the Salvation Army. It's lined, hand-embroidered, enormous, and would sell for more than $100.00 in some of the better New York City second-hand shops.

Books, Books and More Books Books are another staple at every kind of sale. The average price is twenty-five cents for hard-cover books; ten cents for soft-cover books. The charming and profusely illustrated 1892 edition of "Mother Goose," and the collectible 1939 New York World's Fair edition of "The Story of Lucky Strike" (bottom) fell into the average price range.

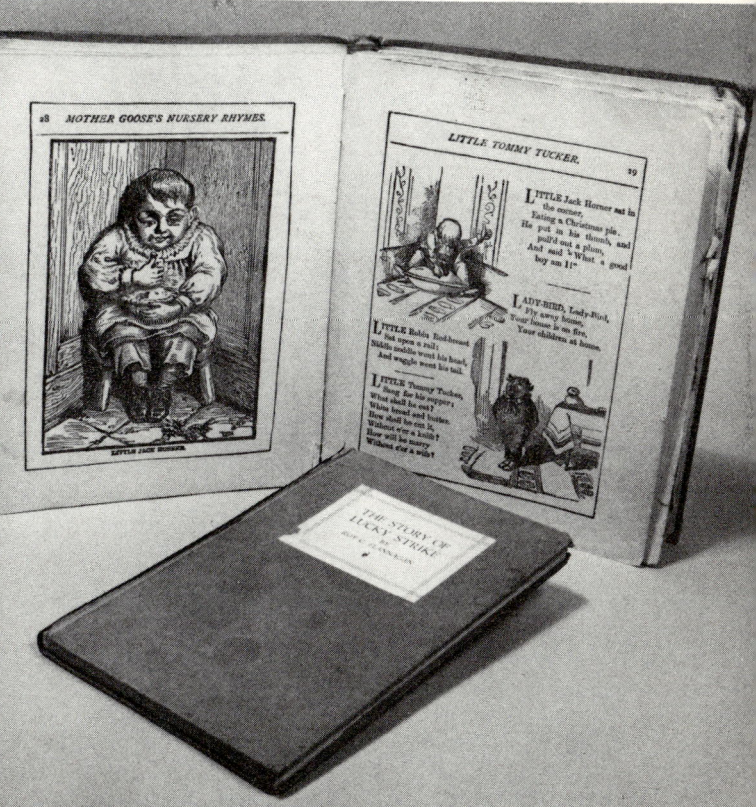

Facing page:

Victorian Locket and Thimble The dealer who sold these to me works from her home, which cuts overhead considerably. The engraved silver thimble was only $2.00. She charged me $5.00 for the remarkable book locket (not gold) which has six double-sided frames and holds twelve photos when opened and closes to less than an inch in size.

Plates, Plates Everywhere I hang plates all over my kitchen walls, and they're plentiful at sales. Just make sure you're not buying the cracked remains of cheap sets of dishes. The larger one on the left is unmarked, rings like a baritone bell when flicked and has marvelously intricate raised decorations on the handles. The smaller one is eleven inches in diameter, marked Pouyat, Limoges, 1906, and has an exquisite border of roses and heavy gold leaf. I found both prizes in a brown bag waiting to be placed at a children's church sale. The price? Fifty cents each.

Garage Sale Dolls The doll on the left is Ideal's P-91 (dolls are usually marked at the back of the head or upper back), was made about 1950-1955, and cost me nothing. I found her in a backyard garbage can, head detached. The owner refused to accept money for her, perhaps because I had already made a few purchases. The Saucy Walker doll in her own box was never played with. She's also an Ideal doll, made around 1953 of hard plastic, and cost me $5.00. She's worth ten times that much in her mint condition. Late-comers sometimes find prizes too. I bought the early composition Shirley Temple doll (right) with original wig and dress for $4.50 on the second day of a garage sale. Probably no one recognized her in her bedraggled condition (I did a lot of hairdressing).

Ice-Age Electric Typewriter This fabulous 1950's dinosaur-sized electric Underwood typewriter, an antique of its kind, cost me $25.00 in 1976 at a benefit. The entire book was typed (and re-typed) on it without a single mechanical repair.

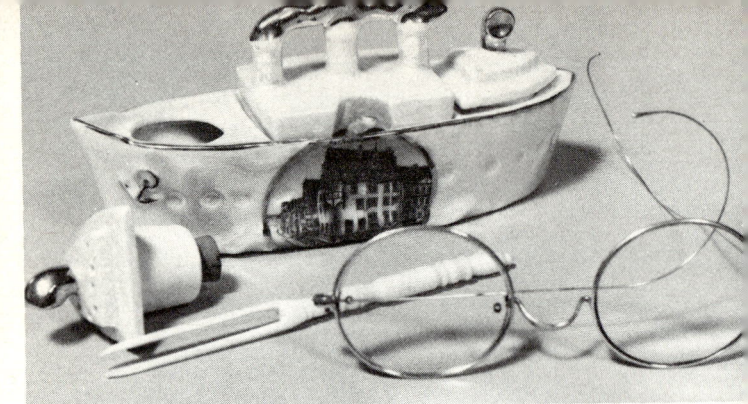

Utilitarian Antiques The old genuine gold-framed glasses are small but still usable. At $1.00 (Boy Scout yard sale), they were a bargain in today's inflated eyeglass market. The small two-tined fork is ivory, cost twenty-five cents, and has been variously described as a lemon spear and lace needle—take your choice. Piece #3 isn't a boat, it's an iridescent china condiment holder—souvenir of Heilbronn, $1.00 at a house sale.

China Invalid Feeders Almost a forgotten commodity, these were once used to feed the sick in the same simple way a bottle is given to a baby—but without the nipple. The smallest one cost $2.00 at a professionally run house sale; the others were $1.00 each at garage sales. A highly sought-after item because there are no reproductions today.

Tin Toys Lionel train #1682 with window and top openings, an honest-to-goodness twenty-five cents (Lionel prices are out-of-sight), at a garage sale. Probably 1930's or 40's. Rabbit pulltoy, marked "J. Chein & Co., made in U.S.A.," seventy-five cents at a patio sale.

Furniture for a Dollar This rustic serving table is fashioned largely of carved and curved tree branches. The dark stain has softened with the years. I paid a smug dollar for it at a nursery school sale. You can imagine my thrill of recognition when I saw an illustration of its twin a month later in a *New York Times* article on flea markets in New York State.

Crystal Cheese Dish This beauty is cut and pressed, but slightly chipped. I found it in a paper bag on the floor of my neighbor's garage. It is risky to pay top price for old cut glass before you've cleaned it thoroughly. That's when the nicks and cracks show up for the first time.

Hand-cast Carved Brass Doorknobs The owner said he worked with the demolition crew that tore down the Carnegie mansion on upper Fifth Avenue, Manhattan. These knobs presumably came from there and were irresistibly cheap at $2.50 each. When I asked my son to guess where his new bedroom doorknobs came from, he immediately answered, "The Carnegie home on Fifth Avenue." Does everything come from there?

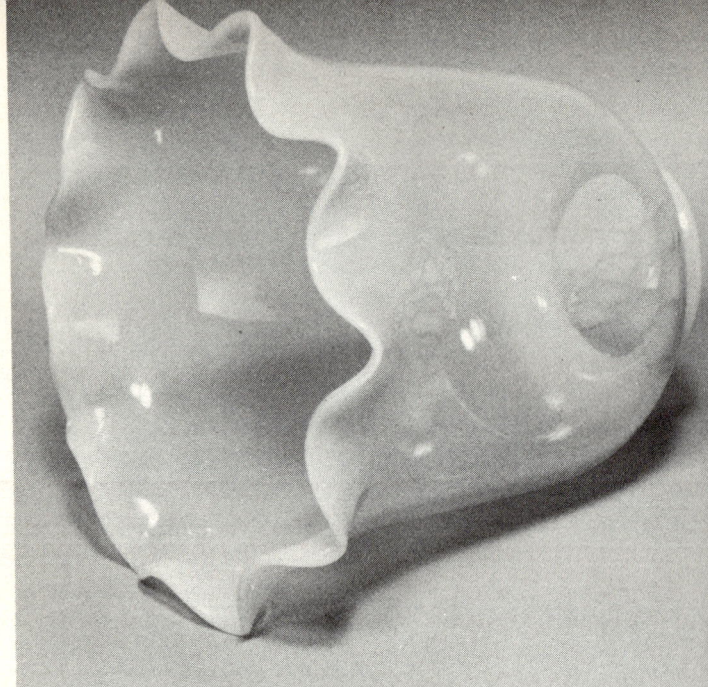

Glamorizing Your Light Bulbs On the left is a $3.00 Victorian hand-blown opalescent shade. I slammed on the brakes as I passed it sitting grubbily on the edge of a yard sale. After it was washed it metamorphosed into a magnificent 8"x8" pale yellow glass bubble. The ceiling fixture on the right is an Art Deco black and white glass pyramid—fifty cents at a church sale.

Facing page:

Iridescent Glass and Pottery On the left is an old purple carnival glass vase that I bought for $1.50 at a house sale but might cost $15.00 minimum in a shop. The other piece is an English art pottery vase with an oriental flower and branch motif on a black background. This too would sell for far more than the $2.50 I paid. L. C. Tiffany has sent the market for iridescent pieces soaring.

Child's Sled for Wet and Dry Weather Sixty years ago mothers pushed their children through the snow with the handle of this sled. When dry weather came, they let the wooden wheels down and had a carriage—four dollars at a patio sale.

9.

Bazaars

There isn't much you can say about bazaars in a book on cheap antiques, other than that many bazaars are now setting up white elephant tables. Remember, white elephants are old unloved hard goods the donor decides she's had long enough. Fortunately, some of them are so old they're antiques.

The next most important thing about bazaars for you, the cheap antiquer, is that they provide you with brand new household goods at low prices. The money you save can be spent on antiques. Bazaar merchandise has been donated by businesses and individuals; the overhead is very low and prices are correspondingly low. You don't often get exactly what you're looking for because you're not at Woolworth's or Sears. But you get a lot of things you can use sooner or later.

Antiques are a little more expensive than most bazaar goods, but they have the advantage of sometimes being unique. I think this is because people are giving to what they consider a good cause and so tend to include a few treasures.

White elephants are cheaper and much more plentiful than antiques. The people who do the pricing aren't infallible and sometimes include desirable antique pieces with the white elephants. This is where you have to exercise your eyes and knowledge.

But antiques and white elephants form only one table at the bazaar. There can be up to a hundred others, all featuring new merchandise at tremendous savings. Most of the tables are set up according to the category of items. These include food, automotive supplies, plumbing equipment, cosmetics, lamps, dishes, jewelry, furniture, new and used books, new clothes, sporting goods, hardware, household supplies, small appliances, and toys. It's like an incomplete department store.

If you can hold off getting these goods at your local stores you should be able to save a bundle during bazaar season. The important thing is not to do a lot of impulse buying. It's a temptation, since most items are going for one-quarter to one-half the store prices. For instance, cosmetics and pantyhose can start at a quarter or fifty cents. I once bought a linoleum cleaner at about a third of its list price. I didn't like it, but I didn't mind not liking it as much as I would have minded at full price. Lately, with inflation, people are being charged more, but bazaars are still a bargain. And since most of them are sponsored by civic and religious institutions, you, the buyer, can feel you're contributing to a favorite charity.

Bazaars have active and dormant seasons, like plants. Summer is the dormant one. The action starts in the early fall, picking up steam toward winter in anticipation of Christmas and Chanukah, and becoming frenzied as holiday time zeroes in. Whether you live in an urban or suburban area you can have your choice of two or three bazaars on any weekend in late November or early December.

After Christmas there's a lull while volunteers recoup their strength. The second round of bazaars begins in midwinter, reaches its peak at Easter, and tapers off for the summer doldrums.

If you want to experience the carnival spirit of the

bazaar, follow me through a typical recent evening, all of it true, so help me. My husband had magnanimously consented to come along because it was Saturday night and we were spending it with his sister Ruth and her husband Albert.

Getting off to a gracious start, my husband's first question after dinner was: "Do we *have* to go to this sideshow?" (Little did I know how prophetic his description was.)

I reminded him that he had promised we could go during a weak moment the night before, while his mind was on TV.

"Come on," Ruth urged, "maybe we'll find an Italian planter." Nobody gets exactly what they want at bazaars, but I didn't tell her that.

"There's plenty of time before the movie," Al soothed my husband. Al's car was a shiny, unmarred Buick Skylark, as virginal as the day it was born. He pulled into a tremendous outside parking lot and was immediately sucked up into an inescapable orbit of at least three hundred circling cars. I heard low moans from the driver's seat. I wondered who needed the soothing now.

There went my hopes for the white elephant table. Three hundred families had gotten to it before me, the desirable items must be gone. Never had I seen so many early arrivers. Why?

"It really is an inflation," I answered myself.

"What?"

"We're having an inflation; that's why everybody's shopping at bazaars."

"Where do I park?" Al's head was halfway out the window, his voice quavery. Meanwhile half a dozen cars behind us were blowing their horns. He lit off like someone had tied a tin can to his tail. I kept hearing the same little moans from the driver's seat. Other cars dropped away from us, but we continued to orbit. I was beginning to feel like "Lost in Space" when we nosed in for a landing.

Ruth was out of the car fast: "Let's go!"

"Wait a minute, I can't park here," her husband decided.

At that point I too jumped out and told them to meet us inside.

This bazaar was held in the social hall of a synagogue. We fought our way downstairs against a tide of people coming up with packages. We made it, I thought to myself as we pushed through the entrance door. We were greeted by a magnificent vista of squirming bodies.

"I've never seen anything like it."

"What are they giving away, gold?"

"No; everybody wants a bargain," I explained.

"I want an Italian planter, cheap."

I certainly wouldn't discourage her now. She might try to leave, and I hadn't gotten to the white elephant table.

Meantime the first thing we saw was a display of Christmas ornaments. In a synagogue? I guess it's no different than finding Hebrew charms at the jewelry counter of a church boutique. It may be that all charities are considered nonpartisan Up There.

You couldn't get near enough to the tables to buy anything. A man on one side of me shoved against a woman in front of me; she gave me the dirtiest look you ever saw. I also, inadvertently, got closer to an unknown table. White elephant?

I tried to see a foot in front of me, no more, but it was no use. Suddenly I was being herded off to one side as two people came out holding packages over their heads. What had they bought?

As the crowd abruptly shifted I was moved three bodies forward and within sight of the merchandise. I had almost—almost—reached the motor oil table. Motor oil!

"Well, no wonder; how can you see where you're going?" I said to a short blonde at my side who turned out not to be my sister-in-law. "Ruth, where are you?"

When no one answered I knew I'd lost her, probably forever. So I pushed off alone in the quest for white elephants.

The next table I got to was cosmetics. I made a mental note of its location because I wanted lipstick. But when I tried to extricate myself from the tangle of bodies I was somehow smashed back against the edge of the counter. I couldn't even turn around to select a lipstick.

It was unbelievable. I had to literally butt my way through the crowd. Here and there I found air pockets from which I was able to chart the position of a number of tables. I saw one covered with canned foods, mostly tuna and gefilte fish. Another was piled high with sneaker boxes. There were jewelry, housewares, and books, and off in one of the corners, surrounded by racks of clothing, were what looked to be the antiques and white elephant display.

At the same moment I saw my husband and Al coming through the doorway at the top of the steps, their faces searching and grim. I waved and yelled, fully aware that they wouldn't notice me in the crush. I could have gotten to them with some difficulty but they would have pulled me out screaming and kicking and I would never have seen my beloved antiques.

No. Let them find me.

I mustered my strength for the trek to the white elephant corner. Dr. Livingston traveling through darkest Africa couldn't have faced worse dangers. I half expected to be gored by some jubilant wild animal carrying home an absurdly inexpensive unsheathed kitchen knife in a paper bag. Or to become the target of careless young dart throwers popping balloons in game booths along the side of the room, or to fall into the barbecue pit and get skewered by its jolly fat chef. On top of all this was the burning hot coffee that slopped out of traveling paper cups onto my legs.

I reached my goal with only one real mishap. It occurred within sight of the antiques table. The heaviest man I had ever seen was carrying an enormous lampshade which, combined with his weight, became a perfect battering ram.

"Mabel!! Look!" he kept shouting, as if Mabel could hear anything above the noise.

People fell away from him like the Red Sea before Moses. I saw him coming, but out of my trained third eye I also saw a little old carved ivory-colored container just being placed on the antiques table, and still up for grabs. I made a dive for it right across his lampshade, and at that I landed on my two feet. But a split second later a rival for the container also landed on my feet. I limped the rest of the night but I managed to pull my prize out from under her hands. It was a small, round covered soapstone dish with hand carved, whole rosettes. I loved it at first sight, especially its one-dollar price tag.

The moral of this story is this: don't give up and go home before going in, just because three hundred people have gotten there before you. Often enough, donations will arrive or be priced late. Buyers still have a chance, even through to the next day.

I stood a few feet away from the table, clutching my purchase for dear life, when two men abducted me. I was being unceremoniously pulled toward the same door I'd entered, but I didn't care. It was a case of euphoric kidnaping.

"Never again . . . ," my husband kept muttering.

We were almost at our destination when we caught up with Ruth backing off from a plant table. (No one but the fat man could walk forward in this room.)

"Look what I got!" She held up a vividly colored Italian planter, planted and ready to be displayed! I refused to believe it. But then, why not? Look at what had happened to me.

"It's not Italian, it's Portuguese. But I figure the two countries are near enough so it doesn't matter."

I figured she was right and she looked happy, even as she was being prodded up the stairs.

We picked our way through the parking lot as though it had been landmined. Cars were coming at us from all directions. By this time the men weren't talking. I'm not going to write another moral to the effect that you should never take your husband to bazaars. Some men love them. I would say, though: know your husband and act accordingly.

The car was parked in the furthest corner of the parking lot. It was diagonal to rather than parallel with the cars on either side of it. It sat there like a gem, unscathed, protected from potential harm by its awkward position. It brought a smile to my brother-in-law's face.

My husband didn't smile until we were six blocks away. Ruth and I never stopped smiling.

10

Rummage Sales

Rummage sales, spiritually speaking, aren't the same as garage sales. They're physically similar but have a major difference: at rummage sales, money isn't a goal; it's a means to a good end. The rummage rightfully belongs in a category of its own.

First, let's consider the causes and effects of rummage sales. Almost always, they're conducted by religious, charitable, civic, or social service organizations for the purpose of raising money. All the merchandise is donated, so they make a 100 percent profit. The proceeds are then used for good causes initiated by the sponsor institution.

Prices, as I've already mentioned, are low, low, low. There isn't another kind of sale that can beat the rummage for cheapness. People flock to it. They're looking for clothes rather than antiques. But the donations include a wide variety of items; and here and there a few antiques will slip through. When you find them (sometimes in a carton under a table), they cost next to nothing.

After you've gone to a number of rummage sales you may lose sight of their nobler aspects. There are too many old clothes piled on tables; there's too much haggling over prices; the room is dreary and the lighting bad, and so on. But you have to rise above these scrubby externals and consider all the benefits: a rummage lets you climb to the noblest heights of nonmaterialism; here you can cultivate your finest, most charitable, most giving self, much as a horticulturist develops a prize rose. In the long run you'll be gaining antiques and good clothes while developing yourself spiritually, a double blessing.

It is now essential that you unlearn the bargaining lessons I gave you for antiques shops and garage sales. At a rummage sale, a humanitarian doesn't bargain (unless you know for sure they're overcharging). However, the price are usually rock bottom. The proceeds go to sweet charity. If you've never contributed to a good cause, this one may be your salvation.

You'll find a few rotten apples among your fellow rummage sale philanthropists. Don't let their actions guide yours. I'm referring specifically to the brethren who elbow you to one side as they crash the line that started forming fifteen minutes before their arrival; and to those greedy standees who surge forward as the doors open, pushing lightweight little old ladies off their feet. (I once saw one of them fight back with her handbag.)

Fortunately these monsters appear infrequently, which is why they stand out. A couple of years ago I attended what promised to be an interesting rummage sale at an imposing Episcopalian church. The waiting line was restless, with people speaking excitedly about the prospect of finding nice things. They couldn't actually see the merchandise because the door windows were blocked off by shades.

Suddenly someone raised all the shades and the line surged forward toward the windows. There were two heads in front of me, between which I saw several crowded bric-a-brac tables. One piece stood out, a large vividly colored teapot that had the appearance of majolica.

I was calculating how I could bypass the stalwarts ahead of me to get to that teapot, when the doors opened. It seemed as though everyone was running toward the item I wanted. When the smoke cleared, the teapot was in the hands of two hysterical women. Each one had a fist clamped onto an available projection.

"It's mine!"

"I had it first!!"

"Ladies, you'll drop it!" worried a short, fragile-looking third party waiting in the wings.

"I won't let go; I know my rights!"

"I had it first!"

By this time one of the rummage hostesses was attracted to the fracas. "You'll smash that lovely teapot," she moaned, trying to snatch it away.

Both women, faced by this common danger, pulled harder. A crowd had gathered by this time, but no bets were being taken. I stood off to one side, one eye on the women and one on the contents of the tables.

Two other hostesses came running, and all of them, pooling their considerable combined weight, managed to break up the fight. Miraculously the teapot survived intact. Do you know who finally got it? Yes, the worried little woman who had the teapot's best interests at heart.

As for me, I came away with an interesting little book, "When You Entertain," published in 1932 by the Coca-Cola Company. I paid ten cents for what is probably a Coca-Cola artifact worth several dollars. I also bought an Art Nouveau sugar bowl minus its cover. It was otherwise perfect, prettily decorated, and cost me fifteen cents.

I still say you meet friendly, pleasant people at rummage sales. The exceptions prove the rule, and they also make more interesting reading.

As for my sugar bowl minus the cover, I have a few instructive words here about flawed antiques, or collectibles, as the case may be. (Cheap antiques are never very old.) You'll find more of these at rummage than at garage sales. The donors probably couldn't bear to throw them out so they hid them in closets and other dark places. Then they moved or painted, finally excavating their archeological treasures. Although the pieces were still flawed, by now they were collectible. Then came the rummage sale. Can't you hear the thoughts of a thousand righteous members? "Here's where I unload this lemon." And they donated them.

An antiques shop owner won't be caught dead with cracked, chipped, or broken merchandise unless the piece is beautiful and the flaw minute. But the ladies who run the rummage sale know they can pull in a dime to a dollar on any donated articles. And I'm one of their customers.

No matter how often I've heard and read that we shouldn't buy flawed antiques because they're a poor investment, I don't care. In the first place, a dollar or less isn't an investment. I've even spent ten dollars (though rarely) on damaged merchandise that I dearly loved. Most of my old furniture is flawed (though furniture can be restored better than glass or pottery).

The important thing is, I might never have been able to afford some of my antiques if they'd been perfect. It's possible to set up beautiful pieces so the damage doesn't show. Then you have the pleasure of looking at them over and over, soaking up their beauty. Don't let future financial return override aesthetics. I have pictures in this book of some of my flawed pieces. See if I wasn't right!

Now that I've talked about rummage antiques in a book that specializes in antiques, I'll move over to clothes, which is the heart of the rummage sale. If you recall, I promised you a discussion about buying used clothing as a means of saving money which can then be used on antiques. The first thing you have to eliminate is your aversion to wearing clothes that have been owned by someone else. Look at it this way: you try on new clothes that strangers have tried; you accept hand-me-downs for your children and yourself from friends who may be less clean than unknown rummage donors; you use antiques to cook and serve your family's food; you sleep under hundred-year-old quilts that covered several generations before you; and for that matter, every time you go to a hotel you're covered by blankets that were used by strangers only yesterday. Then why can't you wear used clothes?

To begin with, dry clean or wash used garments. Most of your purchases won't be the kind that are worn close to the body, like underwear and night garments. You don't have to buy anything that's shabby or damaged because there's usually an abundance of near-perfect merchandise to choose from. And if you're knowledgeable about clothes, you'll come up with sensational couturier garments from time to time. Keep remembering that fine clothes are always cheaply available at rummage sales because the only way some women can salve their consciences about wearing expensive things only two or three times before they get bored, is to donate their wardrobes to a worthy cause.

There's a certain rummage sale that I look forward to every September. It's run by a church in a very affluent community. As a result, the clothes have labels from many prestigious east-coast department stores. They also have labels from small expensive shops. Some contain labels from far-off countries, which you assume the congregants of this impressively architectured church visit regularly. There are labels from famous makers, such as Bill Blass, Anne Fogarty, Calvin Klein, London Fog, Sophie, and many others. And presumably there is a label from God himself, giving his blessing to a worthy cause.

You would think, therefore, that prices would be correspondingly high, as they are in some of the second-hand shops that sell designer clothes (like the store in Manhattan which reputedly handles Jackie Onassis's "gently-worn" high-priced castoffs). But prices are in line with rummages everywhere else.

Furthermore the antiques here are really old, if occasionally damaged. Books and records are of the highest quality. And everything is priced low to sell.

The ensuing battle for possession is beyond belief. I've seen women run from rack to rack pulling out, with unerring instinct, the best merchandise. Later they discard wrong sizes or damaged pieces and try on the remainder. That's the way to do it if you're looking for a wardrobe. Other women pile these fine clothes into box after box and kick and pull them to the checkout counter without a second glance at what's in the boxes.

"Dealers," I hear somebody mumble; "it's not fair." But it's true. While everyone else picks, checks sizes, and examines—always a drawn-out process—the dealers buy by label and condition. Taste and size don't matter to them because they'll probably sell everything. I've mentioned dealers only to prove that values here and in similar rummage sales are extraordinary.

Second-hand rummage garments are usually displayed on a seasonal basis, just as new clothes are. Many institutions hold several rummages a year to cover all the seasons, and there isn't a part of the United States that hasn't seen at least one rummage sale. If you live in a very small town or rural area, you may prefer to drive extra miles to a distant sale. In this way, you'll avoid meeting up with the woman who donated your new pantsuit. We presume she'd keep her discovery to herself, but there are a lot of bigmouths in the world.

I don't know if I've convinced you yet about buying used clothes, but I think the stigma is going away. Young people today seek them out as a lark. Well-to-do matrons are paying high prices for originals from the twenties and thirties, and even the forties. The only stigma is the one you supply when you buy out of need—you feel poor. You're impelled to invest your poverty-ridden, spiritually downtrodden psyche into every used garment you put on your back. You've been brought up to feel shame for not being rich, and old clothes are the final indignity.

But be consistent. You've just become an antiquer. Carry your affinity for old hard goods one step further, and let it change your attitude about used clothes. This is an invaluable opportunity to put expensive, beautiful apparel on your back, and to become as lovely as what covers you.

The shame is gone when you look your best. Put on rich clothes and you'll think rich, act rich, work at high-priced jobs, and marry a wealthy man. I'm still trying to figure out what to promise the family-ridden housewife, other than upward mobility.

Not only do you find everyday quality clothes at rummage sales, but they also have oddball quality clothes, such as my magnificently hand-embroidered Japanese kimono ($2.99), my huge red beach poncho (twenty-five cents), my knotted and fringed South American shirt made up of a rough yellow material that turned half a washing-machine load yellow (twenty-five cents), my breathtaking two-inch-wide intricately beaded belt that I haven't been able to wear with anything (fifty cents), my one-piece much-admired playsuit with fifteen tiny buttons down the front, all of which have to be opened to go to the bathroom (a dollar), and jewelry to go with these garments, including lovely old pins and necklaces for a quarter or a half dollar. Add to this an unbelievable range of materials for home sewing, and the rummage becomes a Persian bazaar right out of Aladdin's world.

But that's not all. The ones that got away were just as sensational. Take the hip-length fur jacket that sat on a rack right in front of my eyes in a synagogue rummage. All I had to do was reach out and pull it off its hanger.

Instead I stood there empty-handed for two minutes, debating with myself: "Is the color right?" (A reddish, not-too-full fur, exactly like the one I later bought new.) "Maybe the size is wrong." All this before I even tried it on. "It'll cost ten dollars to clean," but not five hundred dollars to buy. "What if it's dried out under the lining?" It looked perfect on the outside. "But they'll ask a lot of money for it."

I had all the time in the world. I'd arrived early in my usual quest for nonclothes goods, although my mind and heart were open to outstanding clothing. And then the fur jacket had stopped me dead. I was still debating with myself when suddenly I noticed, out of the corner of my eye, a woman carrying a really old pressed glass vase. I made a half-turn to look at it more closely. In that unguarded moment, a pair of hands snaked up behind me and kidnaped the jacket.

I couldn't do a damn thing about it. In the twilight world of second-hand clothes, possession is nine-tenths of the law.

"Oh-h-h-h!" squealed a young voice beside me, "it's only seven dollars!!" Why hadn't I bothered to look at the tag?

"For campus it'll be good enough," exulted the young woman's companion, probably her mother thinking of the high cost of tuition.

"I don't care how it fits, I want it, I want it!!"

I knew my hopes were dead and buried.

You have to act fast at a rummage sale. And, as in the garage sale, you have to arrive early.

One thing I don't often find at a rummage sale is brand new merchandise. It's always a surprise when I stumble into store-fresh items, some of them left over from the last bazaar. I once saw a few dozen imitation suede vests with metal studs, probably donated by a local merchant. I've also come across new pantyhose, belts, screen patches, small toys, jewelry, yard goods, and the like, all of them unsold bazaar goods or business donations. Rummage prices on these were much cheaper than bazaar prices, which are low to begin with.

One of the biggest categories in hard rummage goods is books, many of which are left over from rummages immemorial. If you need a dictionary, a set of encyclopedias, a thesaurus, or a special study book, you'll find it here. There are also florid novels and outdated nonfiction spanning the last hundred years or more. I've purchased nineteenth-century oldies for a quarter. I rarely use them for display. I buy them because they're fascinating to examine, even if smelly.

I've discovered old first editions of collectible authors, including John Steinbeck and Sinclair Lewis. These would be worth good money if they were in great condition, and if the original dust jacket were intact, and if they were part of the first printing of the first edition, and a few other "ifs," which you can learn by reading books about books. There are plenty of fascinating data on the subject of valuable used books. There are certain books which are worth up to several hundred dollars in the open market. These volumes don't have to be very old. What determines price is demand and rarity. You can find listings by author and title, with full descriptions of what to look for. Ask for source books from your local librarian or bookstore.

I own a complete set of the 1892 Dr. Johnson edition of the *Complete Works of Shakespeare*. These volumes are liberally illustrated with photographs and engravings of nineteenth-century performers, including Ellen Terry, Edwin Booth and Maurice Barrymore. I also own a complete set of *The World's Best Music*, published in 1913 by the University Society. One of the editorial assistants was Ignace J. Paderewski; Enrico Caruso authored an article on voice. Included in these volumes are descriptive commentaries by experts on voice and on every known musical instrument; dictionaries; biographies; musical scores for singers and players; and photos and engravings of the great and near-great in music. I paid twenty-five cents each for all of the above volumes. I paid the same for the 1899 edition of the *Fannie Farmer Cook Book*, which I use and love. They're complete, but their bindings are imperfect. So what? I wouldn't part with them.

Rummage prices can go as low as ten cents for hardcover books. Anything over that sometimes causes a hot argument. "Who charges fifty cents for an old book!" shouted a potential buyer at a Cancer Care rummage.

"But this is perfect. See the cover? Not a scratch—"

"I see it! I want it! For a quarter!"

"But it's a James Joyce book—"

"Who cares who owned it first. Once it's used, it's only worth a quarter!!"

"But it's *Ulysses*, his masterpiece—" The seller's calm had begun to fray.

"I thought you said it was James what's-his-name?"

"Joyce," emphatically.

"So now it's *Ulysses*? What're you trying to do, make me pay more than a quarter?!"

"Yes! Most real readers would grab it—" The seller raised her voice.

"Oh hell, I don't wanna read it. I bought these gorgeous book ends, and this is the cleanest book I found to put between."

"Then it's certainly worth fifty cents!" the seller concluded indignantly, and wouldn't budge from her price.

Rummages follow the same general rules-of-thumb as garage sales, with minor variations. I'll list the procedures according to the system I set up in Chapter 5:

Arrive before the stipulated time. This is just as important for a rummage sale as for a garage sale. One difference between the two is that at a rummage you'll never get to see the merchandise the day before. It may not even be in the building. Therefore, no one (except the volunteers) has a chance to beat you to the best buys.

Publications. Rummages are almost always advertised in newspapers. From time to time, publicity will be spread only by word of mouth (which is effective for organizations with large memberships) or through the local supermarkets.

Analyzing the classified. A rummage sale can be called only by its right name. There are no breakdowns (Estate or Tag sale, Contents of Home, etc.), as in garage sales. It's really very simple.

Rummages are everywhere. Wherever there's an institutional building, you'll find a rummage.

How to bargain. You don't. I laid down the ground rules for bargaining at the beginning of this chapter. Memorize them for the sake of your eternal soul.

A sense of humor. It helps at both kinds of sales, rummage and garage. The jokes at rummages aren't quite the same as in garages. References to husbands (or wives) are missing. The saleswomen are less intense because they're not getting the profits. You can criticize the merchandise inasmuch as it probably didn't belong to the seller. More than once I've heard a buyer remark: "This dress is awful. It smells. It's dirty. They have some nerve donating it in this crummy condition."

"Okay, I get the message. How much should I take off?"

"A dollar." (No salvation there.)

A hostess who wouldn't come down in price got threats of "Where's the manager? I want the manager!"

"Good! I hope she fires me. You can take my place and try selling to yourself."

Types of merchandise and prices. Look at the discussion a few pages back.

People. The patrons of rummages are poorer than those at garage sales. If you're looking to mingle with the elite, you won't find them here. Pensioners and welfarites have always come around for the nononsense prices. But lately the rummage sales are beginning to attract more middle-class people, as well as the ubiquitous dealer. Who knows, the ads may soon read "Black Tie."

Mundane considerations. If you didn't dress up for the garage sale, you certainly shouldn't at rummages. And don't worry about small bills and change; they've usually got plenty. Unlike sales that are held out of doors, rummages don't depend on the weather, and hence aren't seasonal. You'll find more of them in spring and autumn, but they continue throughout the year.

There's always another.

11
Thrift Shops

As I stated in Chapter 1, my introduction to thrift shops began when I moved into my first house. I went from a crowded apartment to eight large rooms and a finished basement. The final effect when we first moved into the house was that of a scene from the Gobi Desert—empty.

I started by patronizing the Salvation Army. It seemed to have the best selection of furniture. A few of its stores in the largest cities contain nothing but furniture. Most combine furniture with clothes and bric-a-brac. The Salvation Army has hundreds of these centers in cities and towns throughout the United States. When you buy from their stores you're doing yourself a favor, and also doing something for thousands of unfortunate people for whom your dollars provide shelter, education, and rehabilitation.

St. Vincent de Paul has a similar though more limited setup. I'm sure there are other such services in various regions of the country that are not familiar to me. You can call the City Hall or Chamber of Commerce nearest you for further information.

I've come across thrift shops wherever I've traveled. They're usually run by local charitable and religious institutions and hospitals. Their inventory is smaller than the Salvation Army's, and prices depend on what the traffic will bear.

Not all thrift shops are thrifty. A while ago I was browsing through the shopping area of one of our most affluent communities when I ran smack into a nicely decorated genteel thrift shop sponsored by a local hospital. With a thrill of recognition, my eyes drank in the contents of the windows (no prices). And then I ebulliently pushed through the only door I had dared to open on that expensive thoroughfare.

I exited ten minutes later with my short-lived joy deflated. No wonder there were no prices displayed in the windows! This was the Cadillac of thrift shops. Its clothes bore the labels of quality manufacturers and big-name designers. The hard goods and antiques were much classier than anything I'd seen outside of regular shops. Donors received a percentage of the proceeds, and nothing was cheap.

Who bought here? Status-conscious ladies from neighboring communities (never from the same town —they might know the donor!) who were willing and able to pay well for second-hand clothing by top manufacturers. So you see, you don't have to be ashamed to walk through the doors of thrift shops anywhere. Everybody's doing it!

Actually most thrift shops offer clothes and hard goods at a fraction of what you'd pay for them anywhere else. You have to go to these stores more than once. You may be looking for a dress and wind up with a sweater, or look for a piece of pressed glass and take home a planter, or buy a fur jacket instead of the pantsuit you hoped to find. People also get wine presses, footpedal sewing machines, nineteenth-century typewriters, hand-cranked washtubs, pet baskets in all sizes; every kind of etcetera you can imagine, all of it donated from newly-aired attics or cellars.

Buyers who know prices and values can pick up many cheap antiques that have slipped past the official pricer (who is anyone who presumably knows current values better than anyone else in the organization). Not every pricer is infallible. They'll frequently mistake something old for something antique, and vice versa.

I walked into my local Salvation Army store one summer morning with extra money (saved from my food budget) and the expectation of making a killing. Summer is a good time in the thrift shops. The competition is away on vacation, or feeling too hot to shop.

This doesn't mean you should let your vigilance flag for a moment. If the place opens at 10 A.M., you must get there five minutes ahead and beat the other early birds. Who knows, the woman in front of you, wearing the stained housedress, may be a canny dealer. She could wipe out a whole counter of antiques as you push idly through the screen door.

On this particular July morning I had been sharing first spot with a man, both of us waiting patiently for the doors to open. My partner had "dealer" written all over him. The men, unlike the women, don't bother to camouflage themselves. They dress normally and drive big cars, including Cadillacs. Sometimes the Salvation Army parking lot in a busy suburban community is as smart-looking as a supper club parking lot. I almost expect an attendant to give me a ticket and park my car.

I was sure my partner was heading for the antiques. I was prepared to walk very fast to keep up with him without losing my dignity or looking obvious. As I walked I would pretend to be examining clothes and other things along the way to put him off his guard. Then suddenly, in the final heat, I would put on my big burst of speed and win the race to the antiques counter.

It's a game I sometimes play. It helps me to maintain a ladylike appearance and fool my subconscious as to my real intention, which is to kill anyone who tries to take what I want. (I still insist that all cheap antiquers are friendly, easygoing creatures, with an occasional misfit.)

I was neck and neck with my adversary, playing my side glance game, when my glance actually did light on an interesting object off to one side. There were shelves in that part of the room which displayed pictures, paintings, photographs, and empty picture frames. I saw a familiar-looking photographic study that I could have sworn was a Wallace Nutting. After a quick glance at the antiques counter—never abandon an objective without first surveying it—I decided the pictures were more interesting. I dropped out of the race, hoping the winner would appreciate what I'd done for him.

Up close I saw that I had discovered a real Wallace Nutting hand-colored photographic print entitled "Larkspur," copyrighted in 1914, and signed, Wallace Nutting. It was priced at $2.50; in an antiques shop it might have brought fifteen dollars or more. The picture was unusual in that the upper part of a woman was superimposed among the flowers, like a dream sequence from a Fellini movie. It didn't look natural and I'm sure it wasn't meant to be, which was an unusual effect at that time.

I examined the print and frame carefully, wondering why it was so cheap. The clue lay in the frame, which was attractive and perfect. Whoever did the pricing had bypassed the antiques expert and sold the picture for the frame only. The buyer may have been expected to destroy the photograph!

I looked over everything on the three shelves and couldn't find another vehicle for my money. Too bad; I'd have to buy clothes instead. Clutching Nutting, I began to shop around. I passed my empty-handed competitor, who stared intensely, jealously, passionately at my new possession. Did I imagine it, or had his face taken on a sinister glow? Twice more when we passed each other, he looked at my picture with evil intent. But I stood up to him, and a little later he slunk out of the store, a beaten man.

Unlike rummage sales and bazaars, which at best are occasional, thrift stores are open daily, and have a fairly good turnover in merchandise. A thrift store sponsored by a church or synagogue frequently has a permanent room in the parent building, which is manned by volunteers; the hours are limited.

Other religious institutions are lucky enough to have a store donated to them. This attracts a wider group of patrons, the shopping hours are longer, and somehow there's always a lot of merchandise.

You can't bargain in most thrift shops. Some Higher Authority sets the price, and the saleslady doesn't dare contradict that final sacred amount. Most of the volunteers are older women doing a good service for the Cause. They've been brainwashed into never contradicting the Head Marker. You don't know who the Head Marker is, and you never will know. I've sometimes suspected it's the lady who's serving me, but I can't prove it. The real problem is that there's a hierarchy of service, with careful count being made of who's on top and who's on the bottom. You'll hear veiled references to it if you have the temerity to ask for a price reduction. It goes like this:

"Oh, Gladys wouldn't like it if you marked this down," a co-worker says to my saleslady, who is showing signs of weakening on price.

"Why should I worry about Gladys?"

"It's her day in charge."

"She's not even here."

"She'll be in at eleven o'clock and she'll close up. Wednesdays and Fridays are always her days in charge—"

"Gladys has been working here longer than any of us," a third woman confirms.

"Besides, *we're* not allowed to reduce prices. Even Gladys won't take it on herself—"

Nobody has looked at me during the conversation. The hierarchy is always more important than the sale. But they can afford to be independent: their prices are right and the merchandise is often superior (though sometimes it's not). There's a wide range, from animal baskets to bridal gowns. You won't be pressured to buy. Most of the old ladies are pleasant, helpful, and probably lonely. I overheard a conversation one busy Saturday morning that pinpointed the underlying personality common to volunteers.

"Can I see the earrings in the corner?"

"The rhinestones?"

"Yes; and the pair next to them."

The jewelry was removed from the shelf and subsequently rejected by the customer.

"Maybe I ought to try on the white necklace."

With great patience the saleslady showed half a dozen more pieces to her customer, but none were satisfactory. It could have been a scene from Cartier or Tiffany, the buyer was so precise and finicky.

"I don't know; I can't find anything here today." The woman seemed morose. She extended her arm in a hopeless arc over tables of blouses, sweaters, underwear and accessories, across racks of dresses and slacks, even shoes.

"Did you look at the bags? And oh yes, we have some new aprons in the corner—brand new, donated by one of our stores here in town." The lines on the saleslady's wrinkled face deepened in empathy. A give-and-take of frustration and the sadness of unfulfilled wishes had passed back and forth between the two women. I'm not exaggerating. There's a certain kind of unselfishness in most people who volunteer for good causes.

"I know what you need!" the saleslady leaned forward enthusiastically, "You ought to get one of our books! We have so many, only twenty-five cents for hardcovers and fifteen for the paperbacks. A book passes the time for you. It gives you company. You can pick it up or put it down whenever you want, not when someone else tells you. You can read it at night before you go to sleep. With a book you don't ever have to be lonely."

The customer thought about it a few moments and without another word went to the bookcase to make a selection.

All the above merchandise is common to all thrift shops. Individually sold books can be found in most of them; the Salvation Army sells books by the pound in one of its New York City stores. Some shops also carry furniture. Prices vary. Clothes are relatively cheaper than hard goods. In larger cities, prices on thrift-shop antiques can run as high as antiques-shop prices.

Usually you can't get exchanges or refunds, and you can't pay by check. It's a cash-and-carry business, with no complaints or repairs allowed. So you'd better try on all garments and choose carefully. There's at least one try-on room in most places. If there's no dressing room, make very sure that you can return the garment within twenty-four hours and get your money back.

In cities and states where there's a sales tax, thrift shops must collect it. Some don't. The latter are few and far between, and I suspect it's an oversight by uninformed salespeople rather than a breach of law.

Shoppers in these stores are usually polite to each other and to the sales help. They're more private and nontalkative than garage salers, but they can be friendly and cooperative when necessary. Nobody grabs. I sometimes wonder if necessity doesn't make us better human beings. Even shoplifting is kept to a minimum.

I haven't said much about privately owned thrift shops. There have always been fewer of these than of the institutional kind. Lately, however, probably because of inflation and joblessness, I've noticed a mild proliferation of private shops.

If you're interested, you'll notice that thrift shops are no longer confined to poor neighborhoods. Exception: for many years a few have occupied some of the best storefronts in Manhattan and other large cities, but these are run by special charities of big institutions. The old-style thrift shops, institutional and private, catered to poverty-stricken people in their own backyards. Both the merchandise and its display were as depressing as the surrounding atmosphere.

Recently, though, I've been noticing privately owned thrift shops in middle-class neighborhoods. The stores are remodeled and painted, and windows are splendidly decorated to show off the best of the new secondhands. The antiques and semi-antiques are clean, undamaged, tasteful, and nicely exhibited. There's also a trend toward antique clothing (1920s, 1930s, 1940s, and 1950s), to cater to the tastes of the younger clientele—and I mean younger, the kind that never used to show up in these places. Only poor families and old people once patronized the thrift shops. Now there's a cross-section of all kinds of people.

The private shop is strictly a consignment operation. Donor and seller share the profits. They work out prices together, and the seller can't raise or reduce without consent of the donor.

Below is a typical contract agreement between a proprietor and donor:

1. All articles of clothing are left at the owner's risk. If they are unsold after six weeks they will be reduced by 20 percent. After twelve weeks they will be considered donated to the shop. Antiques and furniture may be left for twenty-six weeks, or reclaimed by the owner at any time. Antiques and furniture never become the shop's property.

2. Registration fee varies for the year. A commission of 40 percent is charged on everything except antiques and furniture, which are charged 30 percent.
3. Clothing must be clean and seasonal. There is a limit of eight items of clothing at one time; household items are unlimited.
4. The minimum price of all items is one dollar.
5. Payments will be made at the shop on request. The donors are responsible for checking their own time limit.

In a privately owned thrift shop you can be both buyer and seller. Here's how it happened to me one hot summer morning in 1975. By sheer good luck I was first to arrive at the grand opening sale of a nearby shop. I thought I came only to buy, but I soon found out otherwise.

The place was chock full of old pieces, still untouched. There was an old zither, and several pieces of oriental carved soapstone, all semi-cheap. But the pieces that tugged at both my heart and my sense of economy (a combination I always utilize in arriving at my most pleasurable acquisitions) were half a dozen early-twentieth-century Chinese statuettes and planters. They were five dollars each, a phenomenal buy considering their high quality.

"They were left with us by a woman whose husband imported oriental goods before he died," the proprietor explained.

I couldn't really afford ten dollars for two brass planters with enameled, copper, and fake stone insets. Nor could I spend an extra five dollars on a finely delineated white porcelain statuette of Kuan-yin, the oriental goddess of mercy. But I couldn't afford not to, either; they were such fabulous buys.

I had paid for my purchases and was the proud owner of three oriental pieces, of which I can never find enough, when the proprietor proposed, "Why don't you let me sell your own unwanted pieces? Or clothes you can't use anymore? Children's, teenage, we'll be glad to take all of them."

"What a good idea!" I suddenly realized, convinced by the dignity of his presentation. "I'll be back."

I returned a week later with some excellent clothes my teenage children had discarded after six wearings. Adult garments in our house get worn to the seams so the kids can indulge themselves in planned clothing obsolescence. I signed the contract, paid a dollar, and waited for the money to flow in.

I've been doing business with the proprietor—a very honest man—ever since. The profits are slow and steady, and I sometimes leave them behind in exchange for a cheap antique. We work out prices and ideas together. And you can do the same. These days you can sell anything anywhere, without a store front. Thrift shops, flea markets, garage sales, Swap and Shop, they're yours for the asking.

So loosen up; shake off the old mold. Keep telling yourself, "I can." Will yourself to think and act differently; get away from your old patterns. If your values have to conform to what society thinks is proper, you're ripe for a change. It's not easy to wear or sell a second-hand garment for the first time, but it's easier the next time. Maybe you thought it was a disgrace to sell your old clothes, yet a lot of rich and professional people do it constantly. If you change in this small way, you'll go on to bigger and better changes later on, in everything. You may even write a book.

12
Raiding the Rubbish

Have you ever seen interesting refuse waiting in front of someone's house for the garbageman, or the antiques collector, and thought about picking it up yourself?

I tried once—just once—to raid a stranger's garbage. It was about five years ago; I'd been brainwashed by a friend who had found and restored some lovely old furniture from a garbage dump. (She didn't do as well on individual heaps.)

I was driving to the doctor's for my annual checkup when I noticed that a number of houses near there had large refuse piles in front of them, and not of real garbage, but of special pickup material. The trucks were probably on their way. Furthermore, it had been a sparse winter for antiques. I was psychologically attuned to acquisition.

I slowed the car and started to examine the trash. I saw the usual selection of dried boards, old leaves, one dilapidated washing machine, stained boxes, bulging plastic bags, and shreds of furniture that would never add up to a whole. It was the story of my life-as-a-garbage-watcher.

"Discouraging." I was surprised to hear my own

voice. It was like whistling in the dark to give myself courage.

"You don't have to do it," came the instant retort. I was relieved at getting off the hook so easily. My heart just wasn't in this kind of activity.

The drive was suddenly nicer, and safer without the distraction of looking through debris. I was all bliss when into the range of my supposedly impregnable eye flashed a neat stack of throwaways. Propped carefully against the bottom of the pile was a so-so wooden frame enclosing a nineteenth-century figure of a girl. From a distance she looked charming.

I came to one of those screeching stops you see in gangster films, and backed up the car blindly at fifty miles an hour. Fortunately for the world of traffic, no one was following me.

"It's an etching—adorable." They were throwing away the lousy frame so they included the girl who, after eighty-five years or so, had begun to bore them.

Bravely I got out of the car to appropriate the etching. The frame might be salvageable after all, if it were stripped and hammered. And it was old, and right for its subject.

As I reached out to snatch my prize, an invisible deterrent stopped my hand in transit. What was happening? I tried again. It's stealing, echoed the endless commandments of a prolonged childhood. And let me tell you, I was paralyzed. Not even for garbage could I move.

Allowing logic to take its proper course, I finally picked up the frame, but not to put in the car. Oh no, not me. I took it to the house, feeling all churned up inside, and rang the bell. The door opened almost immediately, which made me feel even guiltier.

"Yes?" questioned the well-coifed, smartly-dressed homeowner.

"Is this, uh, yours?" Take the money and run, sang a raw nerve in my brain.

"Where did you get my picture?" She had the look of someone about to call the police.

"Well, I—it was outside—at the garbage—" Now you know my guilty secret; I'm a rag picker.

"The garbage!! How did it get—Charlie!! Charlie, where are you!"

By the time Charlie came she was all worked up. "What d'you mean throwing out this drawing Mama gave us; it's an antique! I told you to clean out the garbage, not mama's drawing!!"

Charlie was as sloppily clothed as she was fastidious. Nor was he cringing before her attack. "Oh come on, June, it's falling apart; it's garbage—"

"Mama gave it to us; all it needs is a new frame. It was Mama's!"

"It's garbage—"

He was right, and I'd just awakened from a long sleep to find myself clutching a piece of garbage as if it were gold. So I set it down where they'd find it when they emerged from their battle, and ran all the way to my car.

And I've never stolen a bit of garbage since.

But I've known of hundreds of people (or less) from all walks of life who have. Garbage is garbage, they say. Once it's been discarded it is in the public domain. In fact, you're doing the owner a favor when you cart it away.

Among the famous and near-famous of my acquaintance who practice the art of garbage-raiding are two schoolteachers, a poor but genteel housewife, an antiques dealer I've met at sales, an unknown surgeon whose brother told me about the former's acquisition of two discarded Chinese Chippendale armchairs that matched six armless ones in his possession, and an assistant editor with whom I was negotiating for the sale of this book and who regularly raids her neighborhood rubbish in Brooklyn (with her father's help).

You'll notice there aren't any disreputable characters on my list. Oh sure, you can still find winos and crazy old women in costumes digging down into public trash baskets. But they're not looking for antiques. The people I've seen picking up furniture and the like from the curbside are sober, sanely dressed, and arrive in station wagons or large Lincoln Continentals, which have enough room to store outsized objects. They stop off week after week, just before pickup time. It's a business practice for them. And because I've become a student of garbage connoisseurship, I've observed the exclusivity of their tastes. Only the best pieces are taken. Defects aren't as important as fine crafting.

I hope the preceding examples encourage you to go after as many freebies as you can lay your hands on in this era of inflated prices. Garbage is garbage. It's yours if you don't suffer from neurotic guilts instilled in all of us by the forces of respectability and morality. If it's been thrown away, you're not stealing. (Make sure it's been thrown away.) If you're a survivor from the dark ages of keeping-up-a-good-front, you could begin your thrust for freedom via the garbage can. And now that I've finished lecturing, I should say that I've begun to eye the garbage again, with a view toward following my own advice.

The prizes can be very worthwhile. I've mentioned old furniture; I want to restate that most of it is well-made. Small objects have a way of slipping into the trash too. If you're lucky you'll find these in separate bags or boxes. On the other hand, you may have to wade through slimy, smelly old food to get at the treasures. Not everything comes easy.

The town dump is a good probing place if you're reluctant to raid individual homes. But you have to watch out for grinders and compactors. They're potential limb destroyers. You may not be allowed to enter the dump while the machines are going, and some places are always off limits to the public.

Other people are zeroing in on these waste disposal areas too, so study yours for the best collection days and hours. Also, you'll have competition from the garbagemen, but they may not be going after the things you want, according to a friend of mine who's an expert on trash trivia. "Garbagemen collect small appliances and such," she assured me, "not antiques."

A friend of mine, Marge, has memorable pieces fished from the garbage and from dumps all over the country. I wish I could adequately describe the charming enameled chandelier in her upstairs bedroom. It's so marvelously complex that you don't miss the broken-off parts. She and her husband were vacationing in the Ohio countryside when she saw the chandelier lying on the ground outside a picket fence. The house it came from was set well back from the road.

"There it was, looking pretty and dusty at the same time. Was it being thrown away? We couldn't see any other houses to figure out whether they had garbage too . . ."

"So you just—took it?" I asked incredulously, from the heights of innocence.

"You know me; I would have, but Ed insisted on looking at a few other houses first."

"What happened?"

"You wouldn't believe! While Ed was gone, a dog came and peed on it before I could shoo him—"

"No!"

"Yes! Ed got back and I told him it damn well was garbage now, and we poured our iced tea all over it and rinsed it in the nearest brook. That made it ours."

Marge spends an hour in our local dump at noon every Friday. The pickup trucks have been out all morning gathering large pieces. They also bring in neatly tied bundles and open bags, some containing wet garbage.

"You don't find nice things like you did years ago," she complains; "people are selling their stuff."

But she has lots of dolls, beach chairs, old furniture, lawn ornaments, pottery, and china to proclaim her devotion to dump removal. She brings most of this to her garage for later garage sales. It clogs her car too, occupying seats that would normally be used by passengers. I've seen Marge sharing the driver's seat with inanimate objects in such a way as to make it difficult to distinguish which one was driving.

One of her most appealing and unusual dump finds is a souvenir of the old Cunard Lines transatlantic cruises. It's a composition doll in a heavy cardboard trunk. The doll is dressed in the style of the 1930s, which includes rolled silk half-stockings. I begged her to sell it to me but she steadfastly refused. Even when I told her she could get at least twenty-five or fifty dollars for it, she wouldn't hear of it.

"I'm sentimental. Whenever I look at that doll I think of where I got it and I feel warm inside."

To understand her attachment, you'd have to picture that little trunk wrapped around with the wet garbage into which Marge plunged the adventurous part of herself. By the time she'd extracted the doll and trunk and cleaned them, there was a bond that a mere exchange of money couldn't have effected.

Neither is Marge squeamish about latching onto housefront rubbish. She's a keen sidewalk watcher, just as some people watch birds. She drives, looks, and drives; sometimes she comes to a sudden stop. On foot she wouldn't cover much ground.

Nothing dampens Marge's enthusiasm for rubbish, not even the snide remarks of neighbors whose throwaways she commandeers.

"They're jealous because they don't have the nerve to do what I do."

"Maybe they don't want to," I suggest timorously, uncertain because of my own ambivalence toward garbage.

"That's what you think."

Marge has a magnificent antiques collection. It covers the whole house—floors, walls, windowsills, tabletops. It keeps pouring in, with very few duds to cheapen it. Her eye is unerring, and insatiable. She talks about moving to a larger house but she'd never do it.

Only a few of Marge's better possessions are from rubbish piles, but they're her most treasured pieces. Trash is an integral part of her philosophy. "If my kids were big, my greatest pleasure in life would be to drive around the streets every day and just collect good trash."

And she means it.

13

Fairs, Farmers' Markets (and Coney Island)

There isn't much to say about fairs. They don't happen often and are therefore a limited source of supply. But surprisingly, it's here that some of the most marvelously old and cheap antiques turn up.

A county or regional fair is something that comes to your general area once a year at approximately the same place and date. It's partially a showcase for new methods in agriculture and home sciences, along with displays of farm implements and animals; it's also a place where people compete in such skills as cooking and baking, needlework, all categories of farming and gardening, woodworking, painting, and other arts and crafts. In addition, it's a backdrop for more active competitions involving athletics, farm techniques, racing cars, horses, and even small aircraft. Finally, it's a fun event, and has rides, games, eating, and drinking.

A country fair can be similar but less complex, less formal, and less official. It can be held anywhere, at any time, and doesn't usually observe a specific date. Fairs are rarely conducted in cold weather because so many of their exhibits are outdoors.

The "fair" concept is expanding. More and more institutions are using it as a money-maker. Hospitals, charitable, civic, social, and religious organizations, schools, colleges, etc., are jumping on the bandwagon. Many of these groups already sponsor bazaars and rummage sales. The fair is simply another name for a similar event; all of them directed toward pulling in money during an inflation-ridden era. Youngsters are attracted to the carnival atmosphere generated by games, rides, and cotton candy; while adults have discovered a spotlight for their skills. Others—you and I—attend in hopes of finding a white elephant table. And we do. It isn't the biggest or most important attraction, but it's there more often than not. And if it's stuck away in a corner, so much the better. You'll zero in on it and have it all to yourself while other people are throwing darts at balloons.

Carnivals are a separate category from fairs, even though many fairs contain carnival amusements (rented from companies that cater to the fund-raising needs of institutions). Carnivals consist almost entirely of games, gambling ("Las Vegas Nights"), rides, and food. Few of them sell products, which rules them out as a source of antiques, so don't waste your time on them.

Farmers' markets also have a fair-like atmosphere, but the emphasis is on buying and selling rather than competitions and games. These markets usually have a home of their own—a big barn of a building that once was used for something else which went out of business like a factory, an airplane hangar, or a large discount store. Although not all farmers' markets are called by that name, there's a basic pattern of operation by which they can be distinguished. They're composed of individual stalls or shops (without doors or ceilings) run by individual owners who sell anything from produce to original oil paintings.

The generic "farmers' market" started as an outlet for farm products (some haven't gotten beyond that). Now, of course, they encompass everything, including antiques and second-hand goods. Most of these places are closed early in the week, but open for a long weekend of selling. If heating is a problem, the building may be closed all winter. Some vendors move to warmer climates.

The more recently organized farmers' markets have changed their format to that of the flea market, probably in deference to the popularity of flea markets, which are the "in" thing of the 1970s. The words "flea market" are incorporated into their advertised name (for instance, "Orlando Turnpike Flea Market"). They foster the image of a London, Paris, or Arabian street market featuring exotic low-priced wares. They go after the bargain-hunting public in a big way. It may be that eventually all farmers' markets will substitute the word flea for farmers, but the idea will remain the same.

Because of their ever-widening popularity, antiques are now being sold in places that never carried them before. Coney Island is one such place. Everybody has heard of Coney Island, New York—the Midway of the World, the biggest carnival-country fair-farmers' market of them all. It's the only place where I never looked for an antique. To me, it was just another carnival: I took the kids there for rides and games. After all, everyone knows a carnival doesn't sell antiques—but Coney Island may soon change all that.

My kids are older now, but my teen-aged daughter Norma still has a yen for merry-go-rounds. This was how we found ourselves in Coney Island one spring weekend not too long ago. We headed straight for what we remembered was the biggest and best carousel ride.

I wasn't in the mood, but my husband Stan decided to join his "little" girl on the horses. While they were going around and around and around (in no time I was too dizzy to watch), I went exploring the neighboring stores—without enthusiasm.

Three doors from the carousel I found myself face-to-face with a dingy-fronted establishment housing a motley assortment of stalls filled with dimly lit, unrecognizable merchandise. I looked up instinctively to see what sort of rubric could encompass the indistinguishable mounds inside. "Antiques," read an ancient, bleak-faced, once-gilt sign which qualified for immediate sale below.

I was stunned. As soon as I recovered I raced inside and became lost to this world. Everything here seemed truly old. I don't think there was a clean and shining reproduction in the whole place. Each stall had the oldest, dirtiest, most authentic-looking items I'd ever seen. I was fascinated and repelled at the same time. The merchandise matched the grimy, musty-smelling, century-old interior as surely as if the two had been brought together by a computer.

I soon found the one stall where I could trust myself to brush against the counter and even touch a few objects without staining my clothes for life. Yes, these were antiques like the ones you saw in regular shops. And there was a lot of jewelry. But no prices; not one. Watch out, flashed the warning signal from my brain. Meantime I was being carefully observed by a very young fellow who was wise before he was born. Neon lights flashed in my head: "Country bumpkin." But I bravely kept on looking. This is where I ought to interject that it never takes me long to find something I'd love to buy. The only problem is money. This week I had a little more of it.

Suddenly I saw a piece of jewelry similar to one I'd coveted for a long time. It was a multiple-strand necklace of small, unfaceted, unevenly-matched garnets. The back part was a gold-filled chain. The clasp was stamped, gold-filled. The garnets looked as real as any I'd examined at other jewelry counters, and there were dozens of them. The proprietor might be asking anything from thirty to fifty dollars, but for me, seventy-five.

Well, I'd toy with him for a while and show him I was as foxy as he was. So I put down the necklace and picked up a few other pieces, showing no favoritism. After I'd played the shell game long enough, I asked two prices.

"Five dollars for the Art Deco compact—it's silver plated, and six dollars for the tie pin; it's ten carat gold."

He knew my game. He was omniscient. He knew I was starting with things I didn't really want. His opening prices were low. In a moment he would sense exactly which piece I'd selected, and then whammo! the final quote would punch me in the face like Muhammad Ali's glove. I had to act fast.

"Oh, yes—the garnet beads. They are garnets?"

"Every one of them real; you can take it for appraisal and bring it back; I'll refund your money. Twenty dollars."

He spoke seriously and earnestly, but it didn't wipe out the crafty expression I had decided must be on his face.

"You see, the price would be higher if the chain were gold instead of gold-filled. Even so, it's a good buy. I got it cheap."

He *knew*. He already knew this was what I wanted. He'd mentally put aside the other pieces.

"I don't know . . ."

"Take your time—look around."

I did. I went to the other stalls. But I was only marking time. And he had me figured every step of the way, that old man with the thick curly black hair. So who was I fooling? I went back, determined to be bold. Which of us was older, anyhow?

"Is that a negotiable price?"

"Make me an offer."

"Fifteen dollars!" I blurted, staring at him unsurely, growing younger by the second.

"It's yours." He handed it to me.

It was too easy. I wanted to toss it back to him for a

higher price. Something was wrong with it: it wasn't old; his mother had bought it at Woolworth's ten years ago—things like that.

I paid and carried it out in a state of happy shock. I decided Coney Island was a new bargain basement for antiques. I also began to decide the necklace was hot. Every joyful day I wore it the feeling became more entrenched. I imagined that the indignant rightful owner would accidentally cross my path, recognize it, and tear it off my neck, as if I were wearing the Hope Diamond!

A year has passed since I bought the garnets. I haven't had them appraised and we haven't gone back to Coney Island. I no longer doubt their authenticity. People who know about such things have admired them, including the man who repairs my jewelry. So they have to be real. Which means they have to be stolen. I'm still in a moral dilemma because I'd never knowingly accept hot merchandise. On the other hand, who should I give them back to? Until I resolve the conflict I'll have to keep wearing them. Especially now that I have earrings to match.

As I said in Chapter 2, most antiques in the county-country fair category are primitives and collectibles. Years back they were called second-hands, and the person behind the counter seemed embarrassed to be charging ten cents for them. They were old doorknobs (carved brass), or old tools (one hundred and fifty years old), or pressed glass dishes used by somebody's great-great-grandmother. They were often buried in a welter of irrelevant merchandise, such as mops and brooms or home-grown vegetables.

Today these same items sit in lonely splendor on top of velvet tablecloths with prices prominently displayed alongside them. Every small-towner is antiques-oriented, and every one of them a self-styled expert. But that's okay. Carefully avoid these instant pros, and shop around for someone whose prices look sensible and whose merchandise is a little better than average.

If you're at a fair you may come across a fabulous antique from a real amateur who rents space on a one-time basis and then retires. This is the person who used to deal in the second-hands described above. He still has the lowest prices in America.

The farmers' (or flea) market is heavily weighted with professionals, business people who know what they're selling. You have to shop at them as carefully as you would at the independent antiques store or flea-market dealer (see the end of the flea-market chapter for the same advice—it can't be repeated too often).

Keep in mind: if you've studied merchandise and prices, you can shop anywhere without getting cheated. You can also find affordable items in unlikely places. You can also get overly high prices knocked down through astute bargaining.

14
Collectors' Clubs

I haven't had personal dealings with collectors' clubs because I'm not a collector of anything specific, just anything I can lay my hands on cheaply. But I've done reading and research on these clubs, and I've attended a couple of their events, including one sponsored by a local chapter of the Federation of Historical Bottle Clubs, all of which surely qualifies me as an "expert." Anyway, if I don't write this chapter you might never know that collectors' clubs are one of the best ways to get antiques without spending money. I'm referring to the ancient art of bartering.

You're a collector in the narrower sense if you find yourself buying more of one kind of antique than any other. Say you're hot on Depression glass, as countless people are. It's attractive and cheap. If you're not young it may bring back your childhood—the penny-pinching, healthy non-gourmet meals, the doubling up with relatives, the hand-me-down clothes. Did you know there are Depression glass clubs, and a monthly publication, *Depression Glass Daze*? The last address I saw for this paper was 12135 N. State Road, Otisville, Michigan 48463. You might write for a sample issue. That way you'll learn whether it still exists.

Depression glass offers a tremendous field of patterns, as well as colors and pieces. You'll find more books being written on the subject than ever before. You can also learn from the less expensive dealers because they handle so much of this glass. But your best chance to learn and swap is through the collectors' clubs. If you're able to connect with one of these groups you'll barter and buy at moderate prices. Club information is available through publications such as the one I just noted. You can even advertise for what *you* want to round out your collection.

Depression glass is only one of hundreds of popular collectibles, for many of which there are clubs all over the country. Most libraries keep the *Encyclopedia of Associations* in their reference department. This publication lists almost every national antiques organization you can join, in its "Hobby and Avocational Organizations" section, Group #13, Vol. I. Following is a representative sampling of these clubs, most of which list their addresses and publications in the encyclopedia:

1. Antique Wireless Assn., which consists of radio historians and collectors.
2. Antique Collectors Club of America. Members receive a 10 percent discount from an affiliated dealers' group.
3. The Carriage Assn. of America. Collectors of horse-drawn vehicles.
4. Chinese Snuff Bottle Society of America. Collectors and dealers.
5. Mechanical Bank Collectors of America.
6. Musical Box Society International. Collectors of music boxes and larger mechanical musical instruments.
7. Society of Caddy-Spoon Collectors (in England).
8. Stevensgraph Collectors Assn.
9. Antique Automobile Club of America.
10. Antique Boat and Yacht Club.

11. National Button Society of America. Antique buttons.
12. Ancient and Honorable Order of Small Castle Owners of Great Britain. Motto: Tax Vobiscum (tax be with you).

One of the most rewarding and constructive ways to make contact with clubs and their members is to attend the shows, conventions (if they allow nonmembers), meetings, fairs, or whatever open get-togethers these organizations offer. There are also newsletters and other moderately-priced publications to which you can subscribe without being a member. If you decide to join a collectors' club you'll have access to membership lists of names and addresses. In addition, you'll get notices of local meetings and convention dates. The meetings are the arenas for swapping, buying and selling, exchanging information, and spontaneous no-cost appraisals of your collectibles from knowledgeable volunteers.

Comradeship is another important commodity supplied by these clubs. I witnessed this warmth firsthand at the bottle collectors' show I mentioned at the beginning of the chapter. I traveled forty miles to this show, and considered it near. The actual members seemed to live closer. They wore badges, busied themselves with displays, supervisory matters, refreshments, and question answering. They knew each other by their first names, and always seemed to be talking shop. Some of those at the sales tables were working dealers.

The displays were fascinating and informative. The most imaginative showed historical panoramas, or large cross-sections of digs with bottles mixed in, or displayed bottles with their type of manufacture, from hand-blown to machine-made. There were bottles in every color and for every function, from utilitarian to decorative. If you didn't know what to collect before, you could surely start from here.

I was especially fascinated by a display created by a thirteen-year-old boy. He showed a number of bottles of varying ages—one of them almost 150 years old—against a tremendous map of the immediate area. He had drawn it himself, and it was a masterpiece. The map pinpointed the exact locations from which he had dug each bottle, and the bottles were connected to the map by vari-colored strings.

"Billy is our youngest member," a proud lady informed me.

I hadn't asked about him, so I guess my admiring expression invited the comment.

"He's always digging; never bought a single bottle—right, Billy?"

The kid nodded, but as though he would have preferred to let the display speak for him.

"How many bottles have you dug, Billy? I'll bet two hundred."

"Well, I sold a lot—"

"Oh yes, yes; he sells to antiques shops. Bill's a regular businessman—" She looked at me sideways to be sure I was still hooked.

"But it's not all business with him. We older members can't take our bottles to school for extra credits in history like Bill does. Wish I'd started younger—"

"Is your collection very large?"

"Oh I'm a charter member of our local club."

"She's vice-president," Billy volunteered.

"But this young fellow knows a lot more about bottles than I do."

"Oh, mom—"

I was still laughing as I went down the next aisle. I suppose we're all press agents for our own children. I wondered if she, as an officer, was expected to vote on displays competing for the awards. If so, he was a shoo-in!

This was the first show I'd been to that featured only one category in the field of antiques. I saw more bottles than I'd ever seen in my life. In my wildest dreams

I'd never have guessed there were so many varieties of milk and soda bottles going back a hundred years or more. But of all the bottles on display, I was most fascinated (in my ignorance) by the poisons, of which there were two cobalt beauties. Both had skull and crossbones insignia. One dealer had his priced at forty dollars; the other, at twenty-two. I stood at a table examining the latter.

"Might be worth the money," the lady next to me observed.

"I saw it over there for forty dollars," I whispered. "Same thing?"

"Looked the same. I'm not an expert."

"Well, considering you can't buy this stuff over the counter anymore, they both could be worthwhile."

I left it for her to buy. I didn't come here to pay dealers' prices. Apparently a few other people had the same idea because the biggest seller at the show was an inexpensive elongated soda pop bottle, which was not even an antique!

The serious collectors, however, were buying, selling, and swapping all around me. They were probably club members who knew each other; who had extensive collections, some of it available for barter; who went to each other's homes; and who accompanied the club on group digs in public places where digging is legal.

Enough on bottles. You get the picture of a typical show, which is just one of the aspects of a collectors' club. Regular meetings are more restricted. There are no dealers operating, although they may be members. I haven't attended a membership meeting but I've seen them advertised in the classified section. Readers were invited to come and bring their wares. I've been told by members of such groups that the real bargains are here, whether for money or exchange.

Clubs are sometimes organized for dual purposes. The National Carousel Roundtable is a group of collectors that is also dedicated to the preservation of endangered old merry-go-rounds. (Some members preserve while others collect, supposedly a sore point among them.) The avowed intention of the club is to keep alive as many old carousels as possible, and large sums of money have been collected toward this end. Unfortunately, some members can't resist buying up and hoarding the delightful hand-carved animals they're presumably committed to return to public use. If the idealists win, all of us will share the occasional joy of coming upon an unexpected old carousel in our travels. If the collectors and attrition win, the old-time merry-go-round may disappear forever.

And then there's the Automatic Musical Instruments Collectors' Association. I learned about this club in an article on player pianos published in the *Sunday New York Times*' "Arts and Leisure" section, which regularly reports on collectors' clubs. The musical instruments club has branches throughout the world. Its meetings focus on buying and selling these instruments (especially player pianos) and disseminating information about repairs. The fact that people know how to do repairs is the main thing that's kept old player pianos alive. The club specializes in distributing service manuals, instruction books, tools, and all the essential materials that went into the making of the original pianos.

Still another collectors' function is that of bringing its membership to the original source of the collectible. If it's glass, the source would be a glass factory. In the case of the National Association of Breweriana Advertising (don't they have breathless names?), it would naturally be a brewery. I've just read an account of their first annual convention, held in 1972, and it took place right at the source: the members were guests of the Pabst Brewing Company in Milwaukee, Wisconsin, and were shown some of the brewery's collection of steins and mugs. The next day, in that same beer city, the Schlitz Brewing Company hosted a breakfast and exhibit of early advertising pieces for them.

Exposure to such authentic collectibles, besides being an unbelievable thrill to a dedicated collector, is a great way to learn what to look for when you buy. If you've seen the real thing, you're not as likely to get fooled.

Conventions have other functions too (such as trading artifacts and electing officers), not the least of which is that of providing members with an unforgettable vacation in an atmosphere of lasting mementos. It's all part of the collecting game and, except for the price of the vacation (which most of us pay anyhow in a place we soon forget), it's guaranteed to save you money in the pursuit of your hobby.

Again, write away to the various publications listed in your local library's copy of the *Encyclopedia of Associations* if you want further information on these clubs. Another excellent source publication is *The Antique Trader Weekly*, P.O. Box 1050, Dubuque, Iowa, 52001, which publishes many articles on collectors' clubs. *The Antique Trader Weekly*, by the way, is a newspaper with a tremendous classified section in which anyone can advertise for specific antiques he wishes to buy or sell. There's a companion publication, *The Antique Trader Price Guide to Antiques*, Babka Publishing Co., 100 Bryant Street, Dubuque, Iowa, 52001, which comes out quarterly, and contains about 100 pages of prices on various antiques.

And while we're on the subject of publications, here are a few more that can provide you with one of the most vital services the collectors' clubs give—namely, communication:

Hobbies (monthly magazine)
Lightner Publishing Corp.
1006 South Michigan Avenue
Chicago, IL 60605
(The Mart is the name of their buy-and-sell section)

Yankee (monthly magazine)
Dublin, NH 03444
(The Original Yankee Swoppers' Column lets you trade one thing for another, not necessarily antiques)

Antiques & Auction News
Box B
Marietta, PA 17547
(Collectors' Dollar Exchange for cheap ads. Dealers often give out A&AN free of charge)

15

Swap and Shop

Maybe it's not called Swap and Shop in every part of the country. But it's known by a similar name (such as Swaperama, Swap 'n Sell, Barterama, Sellerama, Sale-A-Thon, etc.) in enough places to make the idea familiar. Actually it's another variant on the flea market, the farmers' market, and even some fairs. The outstanding distinctions of Swap and Shops are: they're held on large business sites that are nonproductive most of the day or season, such as drive-in theatres or racetracks (trotters and/or flats); their participants are often amateurs (see below for definition); they're usually held outdoors, summer and winter; and the antiques you'll find there are cheap, cheap, cheap (for the most part).

Some of the Swap and Shoppers follow the buying and selling trail all over the country and do nothing else. These people know how to turn over a fast buck wherever there's job lot merchandise. Even so, they're not strictly professionals: their lives are too nomadic, and from time to time they pick up odd jobs unconnected with selling. As for the other amateur participants, some of them come on a one- or two-shot basis until they've exhausted the accumulated odds and ends of several generations of their families; some come occasionally or more often with merchandise they buy cheaply (at garage sales or auctions, for example), and sell a little less cheaply; some buy up job lots (large quantities of any kind of merchandise a manufacturer wants to get rid of at a lower-than-wholesale price) wherever they find them, and sell them anywhere, but they don't stray far from home territory—usually a city—because that's where the job lots are. Some of these people also work at steady part-time jobs. And some of the Swap and Shop participants are buyers—that's right, buyers—you.

There are also professional dealers, but they're outnumbered by the amateurs. You'll know the pro because he exhibits his new or old merchandise with a flair acquired through experience. You could also get to know him by spending every day in the week at a different Swap and Shop or flea market. He travels to all of them; he does nothing else.

There are several reasons I've put Swap and Shop in a separate chapter from the one on the traditional flea market. For one thing, you always pay to get in, whether you're a buyer or seller, whereas the flea market is usually free to buyers. If there's a charity involved, flea markets ask a modest entrance fee which, together with booth rental, brings in a no-risk profit.

Another reason for this separation of categories is cars. Swap and Shops are usually located in a vast area suitable for parking. People sell from cars, or they drive in, park among the sellers, and shop.

And then there's the atmosphere of a Swap and Shop, which is different from that of a flea market. It's unique. Whether it's at a drive-in theater or a racetrack, it has a flavor that can't be duplicated. It's amateurs dealing with amateurs, and no middleman inserts himself between them when the union takes place. There's a nonmercantile, nonmaterialistic attitude about the innumerable transactions going on. Thousands of dollars may be changing hands, but it's more

Swap and Shop

like a picnic than business. People say they have fun here, and I believe them.

If anyone wants to contradict me, fine. You may feel that a flea market is a flea market is a Swap and Shop, but it's my book, and I say Swap and Shop is a thing apart.

On any typical day you have a choice of entering the gate as a buyer or seller. For the higher-priced ticket (anywhere from three to ten dollars and more for reserved spaces) you can be both, so you pay the extra money and drive in.

If you've never been to one of these sales before, the array of cars and merchandise on a busy weekend is mind-boggling. In the first place, you're supposed to get there early (though it's not always necessary; see further on in the chapter where I write about the Chinese figurines). It's still a little dark out, there are no street signs, the parking is uphill (in a drive-in), almost every space is taken, and you're ready to leave before you unpack. But you get properly parked at last, and since you're both buyer and seller you decide to poke your nose into other peoples' merchandise before you display your own.

You walk around in the dawn's early light looking for bargains and bumping into fellow buyer-sellers doing the same. Luckily most people are here to make money, so they're unpacking layer after layer of newspapers while you digress unproductively. You wonder how many papers in this country are actually read. After a while it gets nerve-wracking standing over a cardboard carton while thousands of sheets of newspaper are removed from—what? you ask yourself, as you compete eye to eye for a certain object with a darkly sinister watcher who suspiciously resembles a dealer. You know that you'll never, not in this life, beat him to the treasure lying at the core of all those papers because he's a hustler and you're not. So you move on to a lonelier unpacker.

People are beginning to get settled. Some are drinking coffee from thermos bottles (what time did they get here? 5 A.M.?), and some are placing the last few items on car hoods or collapsible tables. The day is reasonably warm, with little wind; there's a food stand nearby, still unopened but showing signs of life; and there are toilets next to it. What more could you want?

Transactions are taking place already. Since I'm nosey and jealous, I want to see what's being bought. What did I miss out on? A man is holding up a planter from a familiar-looking pottery (not those two perennials, Roseville and McCoy), looking for blemishes. Nothing. Just what I could use for my plants—and pretty.

"A dollar and a half," quotes the owner.

"No-no-no; a dollar—"

"What's the difference," I mumble crazily to myself as I walk; either way it's a prize and oh-h-h! It hurts me to see someone else get it.

A young man is sprawled across the hood of his car next to a display of electronic watches, nothing but watches. Did he steal them?

"Where'd you steal these?" An acquaintance comes up with outstretched hand. They shake. I have a new mind-reading act.

"I got a load of them. Big manufacturer went out of business. Didn't you see the auction notice in the *Times* two Sundays ago? Say, wait'll you hear what I paid—" He draws the other man off to one side, but within viewing distance of that expensive car hood. Too bad: I strain my ears to catch their words, but they're whispering.

A few cars further on there's a display of good blouses hanging on a rack. Three people are smoking comfortably on folding chairs, talking business. I pretend to be interested in the blouses.

"They cost twelve dollars in the department stores. We sell most of them for five. Good deal, right? Wrong. Nobody's buying."

"Money's tight."

"So, all the more reason to get a bargain."

"A buyer can't try them on here. No mirror; it's hard to imagine how it looks. And the label—I never heard of it. People buy labels."

"Take our word. It's quality merchandise."

"We'll try selling them again today. Weather's good. But this is the last time . . ."

I'm not looking for blouses. Clothes don't interest me when I'm hot on the antiques trail. So I continue on my way, poking my head into cartons, examining tables, car hoods, racks, etc. I buy a pair of fifty-cent earrings and a twenty-five-cent glass cruet with a round faceted stopper that looks like it might fit into my cut crystal old cruet at home (it did). The good cruet also cost me twenty-five-cents. That's life.

A lady is handpainting sweat shirts in the next aisle while her little dog Trot watches patiently. Trot isn't the only dog at the drive-in. Where do they relieve themselves?

Painting is one of many arts and crafts I see. Some people are stringing jewelry or glueing things onto other things or cutting things. It's a way to pass the time profitably. And the sun has risen enough to let the craftsmen see what they're doing.

Everybody seems to be talking to everybody else. Strangers have become mobile neighbors. At the end of the day they'll be mobile strangers again, each driving home his own way. But it's all right because friendliness helps to pass the time. There's a background of car radio music here and there. Some sellers have their faces turned to the sun. I feel like I'm at the beach.

"Wait till the real buyers get here; that's when the rush begins. It's still early," an experienced seller explains to a neophyte. I continue walking and looking for buried treasure.

(I finally unpacked my own things, but this is a book about buying, not selling. The latter subject is dealt with in Chapter 18, "Selling Your Antiques.")

Yes, I saw a few excellent buys as I walked, but I don't always want or need what I see. I've heard of people spending pennies on an item worth thousands of dollars at these sales, but these are the exceptions that get into the newspapers. I didn't see any rare, exquisite antiques. I don't believe many of them show up at drive-ins. Anything over a hundred years old (the government definition of a true antique) was discarded fifty years ago or put into the family vault. People bring old things to Swap and Shop, but rarely antiques. The average antiques dealer can find things here only because much of what he sells is old rather than antique. Quality dealers wouldn't be dumb enough to expect Paul Revere to peddle his silver at dawn on Saturday in the Ashtabula Drive-In.

However, it's worth your while to come here for the old pieces, collectibles, and semi-antiques that sell for the cheapest prices anywhere. From time to time you'll hear of real "finds," like the one a lady told me about as we stood together examining Depression glass.

"It was in a dirty old cardboard carton from the A & P, filthy!" Her bosom heaved in disgust and excitement as she blurted the story. "You got to get here early! Otherwise the good stuff goes."

"What time was it?"

"Still dark, and this old lady near us with her hair hanging and the torn apron over her coat was opening this old box. I wasn't gonna go over there because I figured, what could she have? But my curiosity got the better of me and I went. She poked the box under my nose and said she'd sell it to me for four dollars. You know what was inside?"

"No—"

"More broken glass than I ever seen in one place. I almost laughed in her face. An hour later I passed by again; the sun was coming out. When I looked inside the box—I was still curious, you know?—the glass was shinier and this time it wasn't so broken looking; it was more like parts; so I asked her what it was and she couldn't say for sure, would you believe it?"

I shook my head dutifully.

"Then I saw those hanging things for lamps—crystal—what do you call them?"

"Prisms?"

"Yes, yes, lots of them. I was getting more excited now. I thought I'd take a chance; what could I lose? We bargained a little and she let me have the whole box for three dollars."

"And were they lamps?"

"Not right away; are you kidding?! My husband worked over those parts for the next week. I had to wash each piece before he'd touch it! He put them all together without knowing what he'd get in the end, and then he got two lamps! Imagine that! When he was finished with the damn jigsaw puzzle we had two shiny beautiful crystal lamps which he rewired. And listen, not a piece was missing!"

She was reliving the thrill of her find, and I knew I'd feel the same way if it had been me in her place.

"Well, we took them to an antique dealer and she said they were worth fifty dollars each, so then my husband got excited and we haven't missed a Saturday morning since."

The dealer neglected to tell her that since they were electric lamps they weren't ancient. This doesn't minimize their value. Tiffany is also a twentieth-century phenomenon. I'm just repeating that you don't see many real antiques at Swap and Shops—which didn't matter at all to the woman who told me the story, and which won't keep me from going there, and which shouldn't hold you back either.

A few more words about the time element at Swap and Shop. I mentioned earlier in this chapter that it's possible to come late and still find a treasure, like my Chinese figurines.

It was noon on an ordinary dull Thursday. I had toured the cars twice—it was relatively empty—when

I noticed a strange station wagon for the first time. You have to search the grounds and individual exhibits *thoroughly* because it's easy to pass up whole exhibits or small valuable items strewn in with the junk.

I observed two Chinese figurines displayed prominently on the hood of the wagon, along with some fine old plates. Everything here had an old look, as if it had come out of a Victorian home. I just knew I hadn't seen any of it earlier.

My eyes were riveted to the pottery figures. They were seated and paired, the female dressed in a bright orange, old-fashioned kimono, the male in a flowing cobalt robe with a pillbox hat on his head. They looked like a type I'd seen before for quite a bit of money: semi-antique, Chinese export, with various markings, including a yellowing piece of paper glued to the back of the female.

"I didn't see you before."

"Just got here," the woman announced, proving out what I said about time not always being of the essence at S. and S. She took a batch of records out of a bag, and some battered kitchen utensils, toys, and a few other odds and ends.

I put my hands on the figures and didn't take them off until she'd finished unpacking. At a place like this, as I've already said in many ways, possession is nine-tenths of the law! Let go and you're dead.

When I was sure I wanted nothing else she had on display, I examined my Chinese pieces. They were perfect, pretty, and unpriced. I dreaded the answer to my "How much?"

"Two dollars each."

There has to be something wrong; they should cost ten or twenty times as much. They aren't what they seem. Better go over them again. Yes, everything checks out. So what's wrong? I know! They aren't really old; they've just arrived on the boat and they cost a dollar each in the stores. Ha, ha. I'd better ask for a price reduction to protect my honor.

"Would you sell them for three?"

I should have known that simple request would unleash a hurricane. I deserved it.

"I was asking four dollars each last week and nobody had the good sense to buy them, so I cut the price in half. I can tell you, they're worth more—much more! Look at them! They are old! Genuine Chinese figures. They come from an old house where my mother worked for years as a cleaning woman. When the old lady got sick she gave these to my mother along with a lot of other things, like crystal. My mother worked her head off for that old woman, that's why she was rewarded!"

By this time I was fascinated. How many other old pieces did the daughter have for sale? For that matter, what did the mother have?

"Did the woman die?"

"Well, yes. She was very old. And rich. And her children were rich too. They didn't need her stuff. You should see what they unloaded on my mother: furniture, dishes, clothes. They all liked her. And my mother, who's a nut for antiques from having cleaned and touched so many of them in her life, grabbed up everything they gave. She is so greedy—"

"Yeah," concurred a very young woman sharing the sale with her mother (and three siblings), "my grandmother has six rooms chock full of antiques, and she holds onto them like they was gold—"

"Which they is. And don't think she don't know the value of every piece she owns. She consults all them price books. Why, that woman figures she is worth thousands of dollars in antiques alone. But does she share the wealth or even sell a few to make herself comfortable? No way! She works in two really hard jobs to support her antiques habit." My informant burst into loud laughter at her own joke.

"Some of her six rooms is so heaping you can hardly move around," the daughter picked up the narrative, "and what's more, she ain't never home to appreciate all her beauties, she working so hard cleaning more homes waiting for more old people to drop dead and leave her their stuff."

"Once in a while she'll throw us a bone, like these here figures—but only because she got two others almost the same. You know, I'm her only child so she'll give me a birthday present or something, but that's all—"

"We keep tellin' her to let us sell a few things for her out here so she wouldn't have to work so hard—"

"But not her, she don't trust nobody. I think she thinks she gonna take it all into the grave with her!"

The three of us laughed together. But strangely enough, I could appreciate the fierce emotions of this unknown antiques cultist. Working hard all her life at menial jobs, probably uneducated, considered inferior to but paradoxically revered and rewarded by those she served, she had somehow dusted, washed, and studied her way to an understanding of beauty. It was her only compensation for the unrelieved drudgery of her working life. I say she appreciated what she had— in her few hours between jobs, in the darkness of occasional insomnia, in the smoky presence of cooking foods, in the brief leisure of her bathroom visits. I knew her passion, even if her two closest relatives didn't.

So I paid the four dollars and didn't try to bargain again. I didn't care that no one had wanted the figures at their higher price. As I said, they're worth much more. They may not be in the taste of the majority of Swap and Shop buyers, but somewhere there's a market for them—if they ever leave my shelf. As for the dealers who passed them up, those people are always too early for my leisurely seller friend. Which brings us back to what I said before: any time is the right time at the drive-ins, as long as you examine everything thoroughly to be sure you didn't pass up a good buy. Even going-home time is good because that's when people reduce prices.

And also, I wrote my telephone number for the woman to give to her mother. I never miss an opportunity for direct sales which bypass the middleman.

"My mother is never home. Don't expect too much."

I haven't heard anything. Maybe I never will. I don't doubt the prices would be the maximum the books allow. That way she'd be sure to get no buyers.

I think I've said enough about Swap and Shops. Some people become addicted to them, as others do to garage sales or flea markets. Once you've tried them you may never want to go anywhere else. So make sure you've got a warm winter coat because some of them are open all year, and they're bristling with bargains.

16

Antiques Shows

Antiques shows are the ideal arenas for determining the value of your possessions. When so many dealers get together with so much merchandise under one roof, you're bound to find pieces similar or identical to yours, along with their prices.

Shows are also wonderful places to get good buys in antiques of a better quality than those you find at garage sales. This is made possible by those rare show dealers whose prices are very low and whose merchandise is comparable to that in the shops. Most of these people either don't own stores or have them in low-priced areas. The nonowners sell from their homes and at shows. But come early: the regular dealers are also waiting for these people.

Antiques shows are burgeoning into a large national industry. You can find their announcements by the dozen in newspapers, trade journals, and magazines. Any excuse makes a show; cancer and asthma, for example, are among the most popular causes. A school or church may have its fiftieth anniversary—or its fifth. A settlement house might urgently need funds. PTAs everywhere are sponsoring tandem antiques show–flea market events.

You'll find them indoors during cold weather and outdoors in the warm season. Shopping malls and their parking lots are a popular location. These shows are often free of charge, unless they're fund raisers. As I indicated, schools, churches, synagogues, settlement houses, civic and social institutions (by now you're familiar with the roster) are all strong on antiques shows. They don't share the profits from sales, but they collect admissions and rentals.

Hotels and motels house large shows that have fancy exhibits and high prices. But the largest ones are in sporting arenas, and at armories and racetracks. Prices in these places can rise into five and six figures for the choicest antiques.

I've never been close enough to hear a dealer and buyer haggle over a twenty-five-thousand-dollar Queen Anne lowboy, but I did once watch two well-dressed ladies admiring an exhibit of exquisite, ancient-looking crystal stemware at a high-priced show.

One of the ladies did something I wouldn't dare to try. She picked up an intricately blown long-stemmed goblet and held it against the light.

"How much is it?" she asked nonchalantly.

"Five fifty," the dealer answered without taking his eyes off the glass.

She whispered something to her companion. "Put it down," the latter said.

"But I like it—"

"Put it down."

"I don't know, I'm thinking—"

"Put it down slowly," came the friend's persistent response.

The lady with the glass had begun to listen. Her hand came down with great care. Her eyes traveled quizzically from the dealer to her friend.

"Five hundred and fifty dollars," the friend elaborated, "not five dollars and fifty cents. I thought it would be better if you put it down *before* you knew the price."

"Oh." The glass lady looked toward the dealer for confirmation. He nodded a slow, definitive yes. She walked away without another word.

So you'd better stay with your local shows and keep your eyes open for bargains (and reproductions). Even so, you'll rarely get anything for under five dollars. The most recent bargain I got at a show cost me $14.40. Why the odd change? Because it was 20 percent off. I made the deal in the last few hours of the show, when prices are often reduced.

Usually I try to arrive at a show as the doors open. It's the only time you can hope to get bargains. But I couldn't make the opening of the show I've just mentioned, so I settled for the next-to-the-lowest-priced time period, the end.

The show wasn't large: there were thirty-odd exhibits in the grand ballroom of a nice motel. Admission and prices were high. There were no cheapies left, as I had expected—only the lovely stuff that almost no one can afford.

I walked up and down the aisles, covering the same territory again and again. I was determined to get something, since I go to very few shows and like to have a souvenir of each. The last time I'd gone I'd bought my husband a small, beautifully hand-carved snuff container for his birthday. No, he doesn't use snuff. Yes, it went into the curio cabinet. So what? My birthday money also goes into that cabinet.

As I walked around I kept watching for signs that prices were coming down. Nothing. But there were only a couple of hours until the end of the show. Prices were supposed to come down; after all, it's almost a law.

One of the tables I stopped at carried an exhibit of small attractive decanters topped by matching glasses. I needed something like that for my night table, and these weren't too expensive.

"They're called tumble-ups," the proprietress offered, sensing a potential sale. I especially liked a delicate bell-shaped pitcher in clear glass decorated with rows of tiny hand-painted forget-me-nots. It was marked eighteen dollars.

"That's a beauty," continued the pitch; "it's hand-blown: you can see where the pontil was smoothed away."

I said a few friendly words to her and started to walk away. I really couldn't spend eighteen dollars. No. It was unthinkable.

"It's almost the end of the show; I'm taking 20 percent off everything, same as I do for dealers."

Fourteen forty, my adding machine said. Plus tax? Never. If she takes the tax off, I'll buy it. I made a smiling 360-degree turn and picked up the forget-me-not pitcher set. It seemed to be in perfect condition.

Now is the time to make a pertinent point about buying antiques: carefully examine the product before you buy it. Old things tend to have tiny flaws. Look over every inch in bright light. Never worry about offending the seller. An honest dealer will tell you what's wrong with the item, if anything, and scale her price accordingly. But if you're paying what you consider top dollar, you're entitled to a perfect product. Use a magnifying glass where necessary. Use your fingertips if your eyes aren't sure. Put on glasses if you need them. Take your time and don't be bashful: it's your money. Examine first; pay later.

"How old do you think it is?" I asked the seller.

This brings us to another point. You should get every bit of information you can from someone who presumably has superior knowledge. I like to know that what I'm buying is an antique or close to it. I'm not ashamed to say that part of my joy in possessing comes from the antiquity of the item, the realization that a certain amount of hand craftsmanship went into it, and the idea that other generations used it before I did. Who were the users? What were they like? My imagination roams back through the years to other days, other backgrounds, other hands holding this glass. It thrills and saddens me to compare the durability of inanimate objects with our own frailty.

In any case, I was hooked, especially when she said she'd absorb the tax. While she was wrapping the piece, I looked around at other dealers and customers. There seemed to be more action than when I'd first come, so I supposed prices were finally being lowered.

"Do prices come down at the end of the show?" I needed confirmation from an expert.

"Yes, but some dealers hold out until the last hour. And some will come down right from the beginning. They keep their prices high for that purpose."

I still prefer to come early. By doing so in the past I picked up several quality pieces for little money. I only go to shows when I'm ready to splurge, which, translated into my pocketbook, means paying a little more than I do at garage sales.

It's not hard to figure out who has the cheap merchandise. But as in everything else, practice makes perfect. First, you have to arrive as the doors open. Then walk quickly through the entire show, no matter how big it is. Repress the urge to linger over the expensive lovelies; detailed examination comes later. While you walk you're looking for telltale signs:

1. A dealer from an area with a reputation for being cheap. Most dealers have signs with their trade name and place of origin.
2. Type of merchandise. Rule out the obviously magnificent.
3. Prices. When the owner knows he's cheap he'll usually post prices.
4. Lots of customers clustering around an exhibit, as at the flea market. (Others get there early too.) There are good buys where the crowd goes.

Stop dead in your tracks when you see a promising table—one that has attractive, cheap merchandise. Examine everything carefully. If you see something you love, grab it; it may not be there when you get back during your second, slower, swing around the place. Buy it only if it's love at first sight. Anything you have to think about should be held in abeyance, even at the risk of losing it.

This brings up a third important point in the purchase of antiques: if you have any doubts about buying a piece, don't. It's not like new merchandise with built-in exchange or refund terms. Try telling a dealer the piece was chipped when you bought it, or that you don't really like it—especially at a show where nobody knows anybody. If you're not sure you want an item, don't buy it and regret it later. Keep walking; think about it. Maybe it has to grow on you.

Several times when I've been uncertain about something nice at a price I could afford, I was helped to reach a decision by seeing a similar item for more money. That's the sort of thing that makes you run back and buy it. But if it's gone (which can happen during your moment of indecision), be brave and face life without it. You didn't love it enough to begin with. And what about your other values, such as love, family, virtue, country, humanity?

You're doing well indeed when you get a bargain at a show. Many dealers jack up their prices to meet the costs of exhibiting. That's why you should never feel bad about what you don't get.

As I mentioned at the beginning of this chapter, one of the major advantages of the antiques show is that it allows you to determine the value and background of antiques you own, as well as some you'd like to own. Many old products were mass-produced, and even the hand-made ones had duplicates. I saw my lovely hand-blown (but cracked) cranberry glass basket at a show I attended. It was perfect, and was selling for seventy-five dollars; I had paid $1.75 for mine, cracked. I was shocked that hand-blowns could be so identical. But shock is one way you learn, and I have discovered that a good artisan worked fast and productively in the good old days. He made the same thing over and over if it sold well. That's why so many hand-mades are available to today's collectors.

As you walk up and down the aisles of an antiques show, you're sure to come face to face with one or more of your possessions. The first thing you'll look for is price. More often than not, it won't be there. A lot of dealers don't mark their prices at shows. I think it's a clever gimmick whereby they can give different figures to different people, depending on what the traffic will bear. It's also a way of forcing reluctant buyers to communicate verbally. But you can beat the dealer at her own game. You can flatter her into giving as many prices as you want, even though you never buy a thing. Here's how you go about it:

Act less interested in the price than in the inventory—at first. Admire the dealer's stock for its antique value rather than its monetary value. You're paying quiet tribute to the dealer's taste. From there you can gently slide into money talk. You've buttered her up, so she's feeling like a million dollars, and she's ready to give.

Your quest doesn't have to stop at money. The dealer may have pieces similar to ones you bought for a lot less at garage sales, and about which you know nothing. You've already established a rapport with her. Now go the rest of the way: pick her brains. Ask how old her pieces are (the ones that resemble yours), where they were made, who made them (if they're unsigned), by what process, what the materials are, whether the pieces are scarce, what the future market is, and so forth. You don't have to buy; just act like you're going to. And keep out of her way for the rest of the show.

About prices: You have to subtract at least 15 percent from the marked antique-show price of an object similar to yours to determine its real value. A 15 percent markup covers the cost of the show's overhead for the dealer. If her price still seems exorbitant to you, it may be that you've underestimated your own piece. This happened to me not long ago when I came across the figural part of an old oriental lamp I had bought in 1961. The material of the piece in the show was identified as jade. The piece itself was identical to mine except in color. (Jade comes in several colors.) The woman I had bought it from wasn't sure it was jade (it is), so she had charged me twenty-five dollars for the lamp and shade. The show piece cost five hundred dollars. I'm willing to split the difference now that the first shock wave is past.

I've come up against some of my antiques at every show I've attended. So will you. In time you'll develop your own techniques for extracting information from dealers. It's cheaper than paying a professional appraiser two dollars per item, which is the going price for show appraisals. If you plan to use the appraiser's services, try to eavesdrop on him or her for a while—furtively—to hear how he analyzes other people's items. That way you should be able to determine whether he knows what he's talking about. Try to bring him your most costly pieces. You wouldn't want his fee to be higher than the item itself is worth. But I still prefer to get prices through a show dealer (appraisers are or were dealers anyhow). If you go about it nicely, you won't have to pay for it or buy anything. And best of all, you won't have to trudge from one antiques shop to another.

17
Museums

I've made a number of fascinating purchases at museums, including books, jewelry, art reproductions, toys for my children, and other items, many of them from different parts of the world. I have bought only one antique, a small three-handled vase from England equivalent in price to shop antiques. More and more museums are beginning to sell antiques, but their prices are fairly high.

Until recent years antiques were displayed at museums, rather than marketed. Then slowly they found their way into the museum shops in some, though not all, cities. These aren't the same pieces or of the same quality you see on exhibit. Only the best are used for public viewing. How could most of us afford a rare Greek sculpture or a Flemish painting? Even the ancient glass and pottery is valued beyond our means.

There are two main sources of museum-sale antiques: the international marketplace, and the deaccessioning of museum-owned antiques. Let's start with the first. Most museum sales products come from outside the United States, except for reproductions of display items. In fact, many exhibit artifacts have had to come from other parts of the world because the United States is a johnny-come-lately on the antiquity scene. Along with contemporary sales pieces and ancient exhibit items, we're beginning to import antique sales pieces.

As museums have realized that more and more people want antiques, their staffs have picked them up wherever they do their overseas contemporary shopping. Now the old things are being sold alongside the more abundant new products. In this way people can compare today's product with yesterday's. They can touch and/or buy, which is forbidden in the rest of the museum. Prices range from very cheap for small things made of paper, wood, and plastic, to medium high for semi-precious jewelry and reproductions of ancient artifacts, to higher yet for antiques and pieces involving highly skilled workmanship.

I would imagine that museum buyers are knowledgeable and in contact with enough suppliers to get the best possible value on genuine antiques. Most of the old figurines, jewelry, pottery, glass, needlework, and the like, look unmistakably authentic to someone who's into antiques. These pieces are not only from Europe and China, but also from the Near and Middle East, and Africa. You tend to trust a museum piece. It's a thrill to be able to put your hands on and buy a fine old Persian tile, for instance, and to know it's the real thing. Maybe you can even afford it in a museum.

De-accessioning, the second source of museum antiques, is a simpler procedure than world trade. In this case, the museum already owns the merchandise through previous purchase or donation. What happens is that duplicates and slightly flawed or historically useless pieces, along with a few cheap or ugly ones, and maybe some for other reasons, get thrown into the sales pot. They've been lying around in storerooms anyhow. Some have never been nor ever will be displayed. But people keep donating second-rate antiques under the mistaken assumption that their donations will someday be exhibited and make their names immortal.

By selling these poor, unwanted antiques, the museum gives them a chance to crawl into someone's heart and curio cabinet. They get loved. It should happen to human beings.

Prices on these domestic oldies are in the same range as the imported pieces. I don't think price is as important here as the certainty that you're buying something that's exactly what it's represented to be. There are no flim-flam artists out to take the unwary buyer. There are no reproductions except those that are stipulated as such. And if mistakes are made, they're sincere.

As invaluable as museums are to us for what we can buy, they're infinitely more important for what we can see and learn. Earlier in the book I mentioned Egyptian tombs and whole houses lifted bodily from their seventeenth-century resting places. There's also hand-blown glass that spans the centuries from ancient Rome to eighteenth-century New Jersey Stiegel. You wouldn't believe some of the pottery including colorful Chinese and Japanese masterpieces, and anonymously handpainted medieval scene plates that shine as exquisitely as a Rembrandt. You'll also see silver punchbowls and chalices hand sculptured with men, women, and animals as real as you are. Not all museums have all of the above. And not all of them can afford to buy the highest quality artifacts. But they try.

The treasures of the world are stored in a museum. Much research is done on these by curators and other scholars, the results of which are printed and displayed next to the exhibit. It's an education you can't afford to miss. Unlike the information you get in a book with its flat photographs, here you see a three-dimensional object that you can relate to what you're reading. You can keep this in the back of your mind and use it as an example when you're about to purchase something similar to what you saw (it will never be exactly the same).

"Oh sure," you mumble ironically, "the day I find a garage-sale antique which has a near relative in the local museum, that'll be the day—" Don't scoff. It happened to me, in all innocence. I'm not an expert on Japanese prints, two of which I bought at a local flea market. I loved them the minute I saw them, but I knew nothing about their value; it was their beauty that attracted me.

The prints were in a pair of battered bamboo frames, and some of their colors were faded (a characteristic of very old Japanese prints, I learned later). Also the prints were glued to their mats (unforgivable!). I bargained them down from five dollars to two-fifty for the pair, referring politely to their damaged condition. The seller, who was working as a volunteer and knew nothing about them, was amenable to any price I offered. And the owner had probably donated them because the frames were broken. To this day I doubt that he knew their real value.

When I tried to learn something about them—as I always do—all I was told was that they'd been given by a Dr. Somebody-or-other whose phone number I could probably find in the book. I couldn't see myself bothering a busy doctor about a $2.50 pair of prints. They were old; one of them was a market scene of at least a hundred years ago; the other, a water scene with a small ferry boat carrying passengers. I wasn't even sure whether they were Chinese or Japanese. And I loved them, so who cared about their history.

After repairing the frames, I hung them on my living-room wall. They were there for about a year, during which time I never got tired of looking at them. Last summer we took a short vacation, and passed through a few cities with museums. I'm allowed at least one museum if I don't go antiquing. And since the time was limited, I settled for a museum.

As much as I love museums, I don't try to cover everything in them in one day. It's not a good policy if you want to retain what you see. So I settled for the oriental collection, which combined both art and artifacts. In the Japanese section (I had by then determined that my prints were Japanese) I came upon two paintings by the mid-nineteenth-century artist, Hiroshige.

"That's it!" I screamed.

It didn't take my husband, Stan, more than a moment to know what I was talking about. The style was unmistakable.

When I got home I borrowed every Japanese art book I could find in my local library to compare Hiroshige's style and signature with my prints. He was well represented, and described as a master printmaker. By the time I finished reading and comparing, I had no doubt he had both created and reproduced my prints. The only question mark in my mind was why the doctor had let them go. Possibly because he'd had them a long time (since World War II?) and didn't know their value. It's happened before.

Very conservatively, I'd say they're worth a few hundred dollars together, allowing for their problem areas. According to the price guides and some of the prices I've since seen on lesser Japanese prints, they'd bring more if they were perfect. And I insist that the same thing could happen to you. Don't say no. After you've done enough reading, and made enough trips to shows, shops, and museums, you'll have the concept of quality burned into your mind so that you'll know it anywhere you meet up with it.

I know very well that museum prices on fine old antiques won't fit into your budget unless you splurge once a year. But you could concentrate on newer antiques. You might be surprised to find Art Deco pieces in museums, for instance. This is considered the last recognizable art style of the twentieth century, and as such, deserving of a place in art history. You only have to go back fifty years or so, to get into Art Deco. Selling prices for it in museums are lower than on the older pieces. If you don't find Art Deco pieces, ask for them. You may discover that the museum has something old that you can take home, after all.

18
Selling Your Antiques

This is the last phase in your quest for antiques. It has to be included because it's an unavoidable offshoot of buying, unless you want your purchases to completely cover the floors and climb up the walls all over your home. If you don't sell them, it may even become necessary to store your antiques in cartons, never to be seen by human eyes again.

Selling occasional pieces won't make you a professional. You're not going to get a license or a sales tax number. You won't need ledgers or accountants. You're a collector with a spillover of cheap purchases. Or your tastes have changed. Or your fortunes have risen and you want better pieces.

So after a while—and it might take years—you must face your first sale. When you've weathered this trauma and found it pleasantly profitable, you may even begin to seek out pieces to sell or swap.

Your success in selling depends on how you buy. One important criterion is good taste, or at least universal taste. This means that you have to have an accumulation of the kind of antiques that will appeal to many potential buyers. If your taste is kooky (and I have a few kook pieces that I cherish), you may have to sit with your belongings forever.

Another factor in successful selling is having a knowledge of current trends. People tend to buy what's popular. It's like clothes buying: there are actually styles in antiques. Witness the boom in L. C. Tiffany Studios creations, which were neglected only a generation ago. If you can pre-guess the market trends, you should do well.

And then there's the profit factor. You have to learn to buy at the lowest possible prices in order to make money by selling. To do this, you should keep up with prevailing rates in the shops, at shows, in flea markets, and in the price guides.

You may not always show a profit on an antique, but if you've bought wisely you'll almost always get your money back. This is the main advantage antiques have over used, run-of-the-mill items. It's almost a truism to say that an antique pays for itself (especially if you enjoy it for years before you sell it).

There are several avenues of selling open to you. You can do it publicly, which means a garage or flea market sale; or you can do it privately, to dealers or to individual collectors.

The last is physically easier, but it's specialized. One of my friends buys for a few collectors who don't like to do the garage sale circuit (she loves it). Among her customers is an occultist with an appetite for esoterica, from old books to voodoo dolls. Another only wants cherubs. They aren't willing to pay antiques shop prices, so she has to keep her profits low.

One of the pitfalls of deliberately buying for others is that you get stuck with their rejects, including cherubs. However, you have a lucrative alternative if you still wish to sell privately. I'm referring to the dealer. You'll surely find one who's willing to pay cash on the spot for a nice antique. Then, when the item is out of your hands, you don't have to think about it again.

After I made my first sale to a dealer from whom I had previously bought, I walked around for days giddy with money and success. "If I did it once, I can do it again," I reasoned. But what would I sell this time? (My initial sale consisted of a delicate old hand-blown lamp chimney and a hand-painted milk-glass globe for which I'd never found a lamp.) I looked over everything I owned and couldn't bear to part with any of it.

Okay. I'd buy something for resale at the next place I went to. Or the next place. Or the next. And so on. Would you believe it? Not one garage or rummage sale had a lovely, old antique cheap enough for me to buy and resell at a profit. My dealer—actually, there were two I could work with—only wanted fine, quality pieces in absolutely perfect condition.

At least three weeks of looking at semi-old, semi-lovely, and semi-perfect merchandise went by before I stumbled onto a qualifiable product. And then it wasn't just one item, but about six or seven fine old glass pieces on a table at a garage sale run by a woman who hated the antiques she had inherited from her mother-in-law. She knew enough to charge a lot for them, however.

I finally decided on a simple cranberry-colored hand-blown thumbprint pitcher and an amberina hand-blown thumbprint pitcher. I had to dip into twenty dollars of the household money to pay for the cranberry, and eight dollars for the amberina, which had a small imperfection from the firing process. Those were not high prices for the products, only for me. Both pieces were beautiful.

I knew that if my family were to eat all the way to the end of the week I would have to sell one of the antiques, and quickly. I agonized over which one, but that was decided for me by the shop owner after I pointed out the imperfection in the amberina.

"There's a crack at the handle?" She looked faint.

"Yes, right there; you can see it but you can't feel it —it's from the firing."

"This beautiful piece?" Her eyes grew misty. "You don't find much amberina, but—no one buys a cracked piece, no one! Forget it."

She turned to the cranberry. "This is the most popular color anyhow. What do you want for it?" Meantime she had taken it to the doorway and was examining every half-inch of it in the merciless sunlight.

"It's perfect! I haven't thought much about the price." I hadn't thought of anything else all day. I'd changed my mind half a dozen times. "What would you pay for it?"

I knew better. A dealer *never* quotes a price first. She's waiting for you to come up with the amount so she can beat you down.

After she repeated what I was thinking I blurted out, "Forty dollars!" because that would pay all my expenses and leave a little over for operating capital.

She didn't say boo (she later told me she could get a hundred for it at a show), so I knew I had a prize. All she wanted was to take it home to a friend who was a glass connoisseur to verify its authenticity and age. She gave me a receipt and her repeated assurances that it wouldn't be broken.

It wasn't. And she paid me two days later. But I don't mind saying that I had two bad nights wondering if she'd take it, if it would stay whole, if my family would eat. . . . If you're a worrier, don't make large investments on a gamble. Or at least know the quality and salability of your purchases. I was pretty sure of those two pitchers, one of which graces a ledge in my kitchen.

Consignment shops are another outlet for selling your antiques. These are antiques shops or thrift shops to which you can consign your merchandise for sale, splitting the profit with the owner. The larger percentage always goes to you. The advantage here is that customers are ready-made and don't have to be adver-

Selling Your Antiques

tised for. Every step of this procedure is covered in Chapter 11, "Thrift Shops."

One last word. It's much easier to sell to dealers and other private individuals than it is to set up shop in the public marketplace. One needs to acquire a lot of merchandise to sell publicly on a regular basis. Be advised, however, that dealers will try to pay next to nothing unless they have a customer waiting in the wings for your particular object.

If you're thinking of having one or two garage sales or a flea market, there are a few rules and regulations you might want to follow:

For the garage sale:

1. Advertise at least two days before the sale in your local classified column. Ask for the cheapest rates; you don't have to write a book. Study similar ads before you compose yours.
2. Tack up signs in supermarkets in the surrounding area. Also, try a few telephone poles, public trees, and so on. But be considerate and civic-minded enough to take all your signs down afterward. Take advantage of neighborhood institutions that will let you use their dissemination facilities.
3. If you don't have an indoor selling area, you're at the mercy of the weather. But remember this before you call off the sale: serious buyers don't let rain stop them. On the other hand, you might do better concentrating on the flea market, which can either be indoors or put off to the next sunny selling day. What you would have spent on a garage sale ad will go into your price of admission, which is even less than the ad, in some places.
4. Make sure your stock is priced and packed into cartons a few days in advance. This preparation keeps you sane on the busy day of the sale.

5. Visit the bank and get enough small coins and small bills to make change. You don't need extravagant quantities because there are always buyers who have the exact amount.
6. Set up everything in the garage (or basement, or wherever) at least one day in advance, unless it's outside.
7. Get up at dawn of the great day and have things ready two hours before the stipulated starting time. As you know, the dealers and people like yourself arrive at sales earlier than anyone else.
8. One other person is needed to help with sales and keep an eye on potential pilferers. Most buyers are honest, but one crook can spoil the day.
9. Stock up on old newspapers and bags of all sizes for wrapping.
10. Keep the merchandise visible, at table level. Stack everything neatly; it encourages buying.
11. Mark the price on every object you show. Use masking tape or easily removable gummed labels that don't leave a mark. Buyers want to know the cost beforehand. They don't want to think the seller is jacking up the price of an item because they're interested in it.
12. About price. Mark things high so you can be bargained down. It's all in the game. (Don't go overboard, or you'll lose customers.)
13. Around early afternoon, clear out leftovers at ridiculously low prices. You wanted to get rid of them in the first place.
14. Don't bother with a second day's sale. Nobody shows.
15. Expect a certain amount of damage.
16. A cheerful face stimulates buying.

For the flea market:
1. Most of the above applies. Rely on your own intelligence.

2. Load your car the night before, and use up every spare inch of space.
3. Take enough folding tables for your display. Use the hood of your car only as a last resort. Buyers like to look at merchandise without straining themselves. (Also pack two chairs and a sun umbrella.)
4. Arrive at the flea market an hour before it opens to get a decent selling spot. (There are definite areas where the crowds are thickest.) Or reserve a spot beforehand. For a few dollars more you can be a lady.
5. Wear boots, a hat, and gloves against the early morning chill, but bring lighter clothing for later on.
6. It's hard to predict selling patterns at a flea market. My experience has been that the good things sell early, and after that it's too slow for you to bother hanging around. New merchandise is different; it keeps going all day.

The information in this chapter covers standard amateur selling practices. There are other, more specialized, or more exotic methods. As an instance, you'll see want ads in shop windows or in the classified section for specific items, such as old toy trains, or stamps, or old furniture, all of which are hot sellers. The advertisers have customer-collectors with money. But that's a business, and I'm not a business adviser. All I'm aiming for is to advance your fun and your personal collecting capital. If you want to broaden your horizons, get yourself some sound professional advice, and good luck.

19
Potpourri

A potpourri, according to the dictionary, is a mixture of disparate, unrelated materials. Everything in this chapter is related to cheap antiquing, but in disparate ways. The following bits and pieces are worth remembering and utilizing as you go along.

This is the philosophy section. I've talked about it previously, but it needs re-emphasizing. My philosophy is, don't let yourself get carried away by your enthusiasm for something you see, and overpay as a result. Learn not to want the object so much that you're crushed if you can't have it, or if someone gets to it first, or if you lose it through indecision. My philosophy says, there's always another.

As soon as you become a collector you must learn to stifle enthusiasm and/or sentiment. A collector is a gambler, an investor, a businessperson, as much as she's an artist and a lover of fine things. Collecting is a quest you pursue continuously; you can't afford to be sentimental while you're hustling. You're allowed one positive response: "It's lovely; I want it." This establishes your affinity for the piece. Thereafter, maintain total objectivity.

Why no more enthusiasm? To protect yourself. In the first place, you're liable to pay the asking price. (That's okay if the asking price is under a dollar.)

You have to wear a poker face in the antiques market so no one will think they have you over a barrel when you request a reduction in price—which they will if they think you can't live without their possession. You should even tell yourself you don't want the thing; you like it, but that's all. This philosophy also prevents you from overbidding at auctions.

Aside from pure monetary considerations, enthusiasm can break your heart. Supposing you can't afford a piece, but you love it madly. You agonize and agonize over it, and wind up not buying it. You'll be broken-hearted from unrequited love.

And then there are the ones that get away, which you regret for the rest of your life. You're at a garage sale and someone else puts her hands on something you like while you're thinking it over. Or maybe you've picked it up, when suddenly you see another delicious piece, so you put the first one down without thinking. By the time you realize you really wanted the first one, it's gone. The regrets linger on and on and on.

An antiques shop owner told me about a man who had come in several times to examine a certain Gone-with-the-Wind lamp. He never said he wanted it. About two weeks before Christmas he came in and looked around the shop, getting visibly agitated as he searched.

"Where's the lamp?"

"Which lamp?"

"The one I was looking at for my wife's Christmas present."

"The Gone-with-the-Wind lamp? I sold it."

"But I wanted it for my wife—"

"If you'd said something I would have held it for you."

"Then get me another one—just like it—"

"Just like it? Impossible; it's an antique; I can't order it from the manufacturer!"

Even cheap antiques can't be reordered. This doesn't

mean there isn't a similar Gone-with-the-Wind lamp somewhere else. We already know there were duplicates and near-duplicates made of many antiques. Therefore, your most effective method of warding off disappointment brought on by overenthusiasm is the philosophy that there's always another. Keep remembering this as you collect. It applies to everything in life except life itself. There's only one of those, so don't waste it on what might have been.

The process of acquisition is a thrill for all collectors. I have to carry the thrill a step further. My greatest satisfaction comes from collecting cheaply, as per the subject of this book. And I don't mean ordinary cheapness, I mean buying for a price that's way below the market value. That doesn't mean paying twenty-five dollars for a one-hundred-dollar item, although that's always exciting and more profitable than the lower-priced antiques. Instead, I mean putting out twenty-five cents for a five-dollar item. To me that's the ultimate thrill. It doesn't get you gorgeous antiques, but it's a lot of fun.

And don't tell me it can't be done any more. If you're persistent, it can. A few days before writing this, I went to a flea market in a church, which has good sales. It was the third one I'd been to that morning, with no success. I was determined to find something good. The day isn't over, I kept thinking.

I was disappointed to find mostly semipros at the sales tables. But then I discovered a young girl with nice, ten-cent, used jewelry which wasn't too old, and I bought some for my daughter. Encouraged, I prowled around, looking for at least one more amateur who might give me a few good buys.

I had walked twice through the large hall before I discovered a smaller selling room. Out of the corner of my eye I spotted a woman unwrapping pieces. I made a beeline for her table, forsaking all the others. I was almost alone on virgin territory.

The first thing she unveiled was a small, china figural

piece of a boy and girl. Two hands reached for it, only one of them mine. I didn't see the price clearly, but the piece was darling. Was it possible? It was only thirty cents. I stepped out of my usually submissive role and grabbed for it. I was clutching a perfect, Hummel-inspired "Made in Occupied Japan" figurine of a boy playing a horn and a smaller girl snuggling up to him, both of them sitting on a fence. I've never liked the Hummel figures as much as I loved this rough imitation. Yes, it cost thirty cents, and was worth a few dollars more inasmuch as pieces made in Occupied Japan are now considered collector's items. (It's the label that sends up the value; actually the pieces are almost identical to ordinary items made in Japan.)

I also managed to get a seventeenth-century-type male-female Japanese figurine for fifty cents. It was well made and not unlike its European counterparts. But normally I prefer Japanese traditional pieces to their foreign imitations.

The other hand that reached for the figurine got a few nice pieces too. We were polite to each other, which is as it should be in a dog-eat-dog world. But I wasn't sorry I'd grabbed the boy and girl. On the way home I took it out and looked at it whenever I stopped for a red light. I loved it almost as much for its price as for its appearance.

It thrilled me with the same thrill I'd gotten when I bought the one-dollar, iridescent, Tiffany-like, hand-blown toothpick holder, which was worth about fifteen dollars, or maybe even twenty-five. The feeling was also like the one I had when I got a cut-glass perfume bottle with a faceted round stopper for two dollars; or when I found a hand-painted, miniature mustard pot and spoon for thirty-five cents. A very important part of the thrill was that I loved each one of those cheap pieces.

No matter how much love I've lavished on my more expensive pieces, they've never given me the same thrill as the cheap ones. If you haven't already experienced what I'm describing, you will when you make your first coup. The feeling is partially one of greed and possession; much the same, I imagine, as a businessman has when he buys a job lot that has a fat, built-in profit.

Now I'm going to talk about larceny. You have to have a small streak of it to grab good things for less money than they're worth. What!! Me, larcenous? Yes, or I would have handed back all those lovely things to their owners and told them they could easily get dollars more for them. I myself have paid high prices for things I wanted very much and couldn't get at a lower price.

The choice is larceny or total abnegation. But if I give up my cheap antiques I'll lose a great pleasure, a way of life. I don't have enough money for the more expensive pieces, except when I scrimp and save, as I sometimes do. And *that's* no fun.

What's the solution? To rationalize. You tell yourself that if you didn't buy these things cheaply, someone else would, and the seller would still be out of luck. You tell yourself that some people set no value whatsoever on old things. They're glad to get rid of them and be paid anything at all. You tell yourself that if something infinitely valuable came your way you'd turn it down and put the seller wise. (How lucky that I didn't discover the Hiroshiges until a year after I'd bought them.)

Now it's your turn to think of a rationalization.

Reproductions are a very tricky aspect of antique buying. They've been known to fool the experts, so what chance do you stand? The most important thing in your favor is that you're buying cheap antiques. Reproductions are usually modeled on the highest quality, expensive antiques that date from a much earlier period than those you're buying. They are reproduced because they're scarce and highly sought after.

But don't lull yourself into inertia. Be alert. That's

how you catch the villain. Get to know the look and patina of old things. Then go into the stores and compare the old look with the new. Whether it's glass, furniture, or anything else, you'll soon know the difference between the two. And while you're in the stores, examine the brand new reproductions. Here you'll find both expensive and cheap ones. Study them. Impress them on your mind. Look at the marks on the bottom. Look for other telltale signs of newness. These are your defenses when you visit your next antique shop. For it's there, rather than in the garage sales, that you'll find the reproductions deliberately sold as antiques. Let the buyer beware, if you don't know the dealer.

At a garage or rummage sale, you're not spending enough money for it to hurt if you make a mistake and buy a reproduction, thinking it's an antique.

Finally, can a reproduction be an antique? Yes, if it was made more than a hundred years ago. The Victorians, in addition to creating their own styles, also copied earlier periods. Such copies should be labeled for what they are, and priced accordingly. Unfortunately, whether by intent or by honest mistake, many of these are sold as originals, and richer people than you are paying through the nose for them.

Additional notes:

Look over your potential purchase in broad daylight. Garage or house interiors are usually dark. Put on your glasses if you need them. Take the piece to a bright window or outside the door, where the light will show up faint chips, cracks, discolorations, and the like. This is the best way to uncover damages.

Read. Yes, I've said it before, and you're bored with hearing it. But you should learn about antiques before you buy, not after. If you can't easily get to the shops and museums (or if the unattainability of their contents frustrates you), then go to your local library. Buy a book instead of an antique. Look at loads of photographs. That's how you learn what's genuinely old when you're unable to touch the objects.

After reading, *see and touch* as much as possible. These too are important in determining a true antique.

Digging is a very important aspect of your search for antiques. At sales, things are often piled up high or stored under tables for lack of room. You may have to pull unpacked boxes into the light of day and open them yourself. I'm reminded of the aphorism I once saw outside a church: things turn up for the man who digs. So don't be bashful.

Repairs are included here only because they may make the difference between buying and not buying an antique. Are you going to pass up a once beautiful, now slightly battered, old piece because the market dictates that it be in mint condition? If you can buy this battered beauty at its bottom price, you may be able to restore it to its former glory for little money.

There are two types of repairs, the kind you have done by professionals, and the kind you do yourself. If you want something done by an expert, I believe in going right to the source: other collectors and antiques shop owners. Both know the best and cheapest repair people, so why should you go through trial and error? I've found that many shop owners are willing to share their list of craftsmen, especially if you're an occasional buyer.

Don't underestimate your do-it-yourself abilities. With twin-tube epoxy cement you can repair almost anything. Follow the instructions carefully, especially when it comes to clamping, which can be done with anything from rubber bands to rope. This procedure is great for china, glass, jewelry, metals, you name it. The repair will hold up interminably, washing after washing (except in automatic dishwashers), although you can always see a line where it's mended. You need a pro if you want an undetectable job.

Badly faded, soiled, or discolored pieces can be restored if you sit them in a pool of bleach or dishwasher detergent overnight. There are also more drastic methods, but you'll have to look these up in your local library books.

I swear by the cheap hobby paints for touching up lightly chipped plate edges. Sometimes you can flesh out the chip first by adding a few dabs of doll cement or white semi-liquid porcelain mender, for instance. These menders are also good on cracks inside the plates.

Cleaning antiques. The best furniture cleaners are the tried and true ones, from standard old commercial polishes to grandma's home recipe. Lemon or linseed oils are good, if used sparingly. Don't experiment on fine antiques with untried products.

Don't put old china in your dishwasher. One cycle may remove the decoration. However, there are exceptions. I have a beautiful (inherited) set of sixty-four-year-old Vignaud Limoges dishes, but I hated the thought of washing each one by hand. So—I decided to experiment with one broken plate in the dishwasher. I kept it there every day for the next two months; not a single rose changed color. It was an early dishwasher-proof china, which undoubtedly has something to do with the way it was fired. Try this yourself.

I use a very effective home recipe for silver: I mix whiting and rubbing alcohol to a semi-thick paste. I've used milk on ivory piano keys with good results. I've soaked old materials (except lace) in soap suds or in pre-soak laundry detergent, and gotten fabulous results with both. Stubborn stains sometimes don't yield to mild soap. If you work with the strong stuff, watch over it carefully.

The subject of repairs and cleansers needs a book unto itself, and many have been written. Go to your library, read carefully, follow instructions, and your reward will be new vistas in crummy, gummy, faded, and broken antiques; to me, ever a delightful combination.